TURNING POINTS

A Journey through Challenges

A.P.J. Abdul Kalam

HarperCollins *Publishers* India
a joint venture with

New Delhi

First published in India in 2012 by
HarperCollins *Publishers* India
a joint venture with
The India Today Group

Copyright © A.P.J. Abdul Kalam 2012

ISBN: 978-93-5029-347-8

6 8 10 9 7 5

HarperCollins *Publishers*
A-53, Sector 57, Noida, Uttar Pradesh 201301, India
77-85 Fulham Palace Road, London W6 8JB, United Kingdom
Hazelton Lanes, 55 Avenue Road, Suite 2900, Toronto, Ontario M5R 3L2
and 1995 Markham Road, Scarborough, Ontario M1B 5M8, Canada
25 Ryde Road, Pymble, Sydney, NSW 2073, Australia
31 View Road, Glenfield, Auckland 10, New Zealand
10 East 53rd Street, New York NY 10022, USA

Typeset in 13/15 Garamond Regular at
SÜRYA

Printed and bound at
Thomson Press (India) Ltd.

CONTENTS

TURNING POINTS

AVUL PAKIR JAINULABDEEN ABDUL KALAM was the eleventh President of India, from 2002 to 2007. He is a recipient of the Padma Bhushan, the Padma Vibhushan and the nation's highest civilian award, the Bharat Ratna.

Born in 1931 in Rameswaram in Tamil Nadu, Dr Kalam studied aeronautical engineering at the Madras Institute of Technology. He played a key role in the development of India's first satellite launch vehicle, the SLV-3, which launched the Rohini satellite in 1980 to take India into the space club; in the building and operationalization of India's strategic missile systems; and in the 1998 nuclear tests. As chairman of the Technology Information, Forecasting and Assessment Council (TIFAC) and as an eminent scientist, he led the country with the help of 500 experts to arrive at Technology Vision 2020 giving a road map for transforming India into a developed nation.

As an elder statesman, he remains in the public eye for his role in offering counsel, reaching out to people and building bridges across religious and social divides. Dr Kalam's focus stays on transforming India into a developed nation by 2020 and to this end he continues to follow a rigorous schedule that has him travelling across the country for his teaching assignments at IITs and IIMs, to address conferences and to meet students and people from all walks of life.

PREFACE

My book *Wings of Fire* covered my life up to 1992. Ever since it was published in 1999 the response has been astounding and the book has sold more than a million copies. More heartening still is that it appears to have made a positive impact on thousands of people, helping them change their lives for the better.

As I wrote *Turning Points* the thought occurred to me why I was writing the book. One could say that my story echoes the concerns, anxieties and aspirations of many Indians. Like them I started my life from the lowest step in the ladder. My first job was as senior scientific assistant. Gradually I moved up to greater responsibilities, finally assuming the office of the president of India. Certainly much has happened in the past decade and more which needs recounting. One could say that it has been a very intense experience.

However, my reasons for writing *Turning Points* were slightly different. Seeing the response generated by *Wings of Fire* I felt that if in the same way this book too could benefit a few people it would be well worth the effort. In fact, if even one person or one family find their life changing for the better because of something gleaned from this book, I will feel fulfilled. Hence this book for you, dear reader.

30 May 2012   A.P.J. ABDUL KALAM
New Delhi

ACKNOWLEDGEMENTS

Dear Friends, I am eighty years of age, and have just completed my twenty-first book – *Turning Points*. It all started one winter morning at my residence at 10 Rajaji Marg, New Delhi. I and H. Sheridon, my personal secretary, were going through my diaries and we found that there were seven turning points or challenges – eight if you include life after demitting the office of president – navigating which made me succeed in life.

I am full of gratitude to the people who have poured out their love and affection to me throughout my life. As also to those who have shared their challenges and happiness with me. I would add to this number the readers of my books, two of which have reached more than a million readers, and five others have found more than a 100,000 readers. I am deeply grateful to all. Particularly, one person whom I would like to convey my heartiest gratitude to is Major General R. Swaminathan, who has been with me for more than thirty years, during all the phases of my life in many successes and a few failures. He is a friend, philosopher and guide. He played a very important role in bringing out *Turning Points* making sure to maintain the utmost accuracy in the details.

The book would not have taken shape without the untiring and dedicated efforts of Dhan Shyam Sharma and Vishal Rastogi in the preparation of the manuscript. I value the fine inputs given by Narayana Moorthy and V. Ponraj. I am deeply indebted to Krishan Chopra of HarperCollins for his great contribution in reviewing the manuscript and structuring the book through his constant interaction with me and carrying out meticulous editing. I also thank Rajinder Ganju, who went out of his way in typesetting the whole manuscript in a very short time to help take the book through to press.

1

WHEN CAN I SING A SONG OF INDIA?

Keep loving nature and care for its blessings
Then you can see divinity all over

It was 24 July 2007, the last day of my presidency. It was a day filled with many engagements. In the morning I was busy with personal work. Later in the day, starting from 3.25 p.m., there was a short interview with Rajdeep Sardesai and Dilip Venkatraman from CNN-IBN, followed by a meeting with E.S.L. Narasimhan, governor of Chhattisgarh. After this I was to meet Dr Ramesh Pokhariyal 'Nishank', minister of health and family welfare and science and technology, Uttarakhand. There was a meeting with Ms Charishma Thankappan, a student of Delhi's Hindu College, along with her parents and five others, and then at 4.00 p.m. with Sunil Lal, chief of protocol, Ministry of External Affairs, along with his wife, Gitanjali, and their daughter, Nitika. And so it went with several other farewell calls until 8 p.m., when I was to host a dinner for the President-elect, the Vice President, the Prime Minister and the Council of Ministers.

In all the round of farewells and meeting callers, speaking to friends and seeing to it that my few belongings were packed – the two suitcases, so to say, that I had said was all I would take away with me – there was an unspoken thought that was in the air. Whosoever met me or talked to me had one question uppermost in their mind: What would I be doing? Had I worked it out? Would I go back to teaching? Would I retire from active life? Unlikely as this last was to anyone who knows me. For now the last five years at Rashtrapati Bhavan were fresh in my mind. The welcoming flowers of the Mughal Garden, where Ustad Bismillah Khan gave his last performance and many other musicians also performed, the fragrance of the herbal gardens, the dancing peacocks, the guards who stood alert under the hot summer sun and in the biting cold of winter – all had become part of my daily life. What a rich experience these five years had been!

People from every field and walk of life had poured out their ideas for the development of the nation to me. They vied with each other to tell me how they had contributed their mite. Politicians at every level shared their vision for developing their constituencies. Scientists showed their hunger to help solve pressing issues. Artists and writers expressed eloquently their love for India. Religious leaders shared a common platform to speak on spiritual harmony and unity of minds. Specialists from different fields shared their thoughts on building a knowledge society. The legal and judicial communities frequently offered their ideas on many current topics like fair treatment for all citizens, fast-track disposal of cases and e-judiciary. The non-resident Indians whenever they met me, showed a desire to give back to the country of their birth whatever they could to see it develop and improve.

My visits to different parts of the country always provided me with unique experiences, which made me understand the aspirations of the people, the good work done by many, and above all, the power of the youth.

My interaction with the medical fraternity was wide-ranging, be it in their efforts to extend affordable medical care to every rural citizen, encourage research, ease the life of differently abled people, promote the care of senior citizens or spread the message of lifestyle changes for preventive health care. Nurses who met me both in India and abroad volunteered to set up centres of high quality care, particularly for people in villages.

My interactions with farmers, including cotton farmers in distress, enabled me to understand the problems and challenges they face and helped me formulate and convey my ideas to agricultural scientists.

My meeting with postmen triggered the thought that the

postal system could play a pivotal role in a knowledge society with postmen becoming knowledge officers in rural areas.

Policemen met me and gave their ideas on police reforms, improving police station infrastructure and the application of information technology to police functioning, ideas which I could share in the forum considering police reforms.

The panchayat presidents, particularly the women presidents, explained their plans and programmes for improving their villages and the hurdles they faced.

Wherever I went, teachers assured me that their mission was to groom the youth for nation building. They would strive to impart values to the young which would help them become enlightened citizens, they said.

All these enriching experiences culminated in the design of oaths, which summarized the desirable actions to be taken by each segment of the society, whether it be children, parents, teachers, Servicemen, administrators, lawyers, doctors, nurses, or others. The administration of the oaths became part of the interaction with different groups of people. Generally these oaths comprised five, seven or ten points pertinent to that section of society. The gatherings were normally large, and the recitation of these oaths brought the entire audience together in a common purpose and conveyed a message that they could all carry with them through their lives.

One of the features that never ceased to astonish me was the sheer volume of letters, emails and other correspondence that used to arrive while I was president. The letters were from children, youth, adults, teachers, scientists – just about everyone. Unbelievably, there were thousands of letters every day. It was not possible to answer all the queries or to provide the kind of help required. But we tried. In many cases we forwarded the letters to the officials concerned for further action. If it was for medical treatment we tried to suggest a suitable hospital. At other times we pitched in with advice or suggestions ourselves. Even at times with a small monetary assistance. It was astonishing how in all the optimism, faith and hope that the letters showed our countrymen as possessing, there were also these vast islands of suffering, pain and destitution. One letter that touched me came from a young girl whose family was in straitened circumstances. Somewhere in that haunting letter I sensed a spirit and an ability to change her life for the better. We forwarded her letter to someone we thought might be able to help, with surprising consequences.

'My family is in trouble. My family is facing problems from 23 years. There is not a single day when I and my family never saw a single happy moment. I was good in studies. I stand first from my center in 5th class. I want to became a doctor. But after that I never got first stand. I always got second or third place. In my B.A. I only got 50%. I could not join medical because I always feel stress. I am in stress for 14 years . . .'

There were many such letters. It was touching to see the faith they showed in the ability of the President's Office to help, and their honesty and complete lack of guile.

In contrast were the letters from various associations and institutions. 'Dear President Kalam, we are hosting a conference on advanced nanotechnology (or some other specialized subject, such as biodiversity, carbon composites, rocket propulsion technology, cardiothoracic surgery, infectious diseases, strategy for reducing pendency of court cases, or e-governance) and we would like you to deliver the keynote address . . .' These of course were much easier to answer. It was just a matter of dates, and my knowledge of the subject. Both that young girl looking for an opportunity to do well in life and these conferences on cutting-edge technology were two facets that needed to be addressed for India 2020.

With these thoughts, I asked myself what I should do next. Should I merely put down my reminiscences or was there something else I could do? It was not easy to decide. One key event that day made my job a little easier – the preparation for my farewell address to the nation.

I decided that I should in my address thank the citizens and share the development profile for India, which had been evolved with them and for them over the last five years.

In essence, I told them, My dear citizens, let us resolve to continue to work towards realizing the mission of a country that is prosperous, healthy, secure, peaceful and happy and continues on a sustainable growth path, where the rural and urban divide has been reduced to a thin line and where the governance is responsive, transparent and corruption-free. There were some other points in the ten-point profile for a developed India that I drew up, which I list further on in the book.

This then remains my mission in life: to connect the billion hearts and minds of the people of India in our multicultural society through the ten pillars of development and to embed the self-confidence that 'we can do it'. I will always be with you, dear citizens, in the great mission of making India a developed nation before 2020.

Here are a few events that lightened my horizon, brought a smile to my lips, taught me lessons and engaged me with the love of my countrymen.

2

MY NINTH LECTURE AT ANNA UNIVERSITY

The ignited mind of the youth is
the most powerful resource
on the earth, above the earth
and under the earth

A yellow bird sings on the jamun tree and makes my morning walk a pleasure. I keep a lookout for the pair of hornbills that sometimes drift into my garden. Ten Rajaji Marg is my abode after Rashtrapati Bhavan. I am told that it once housed Edwin Lutyens, the architect of New Delhi.

Time passes like the wind, keeping me busy in teaching and research in India and abroad. The enthusiasm and resolve on the young faces I see in the classrooms gives me energy too.

The last few years have demonstrated to me the passionate desire of the people to realize the mission of a developed India and their commitment to contribute whatever they can. As I think back and revisit my presidential days some key events come to mind. The events represent the diverse characteristics of this diverse country, with its glorious past and challenging present. But one message is clear: India will be a developed nation by 2020.

∼

The morning of 10 June 2002 was like any other day in the beautiful environment of Anna University, where I had been working since December 2001. I had been enjoying my time in the large, tranquil campus, working with professors and inquisitive students on research projects and teaching. The authorized strength of my class was sixty students, but during every lecture, the classroom had more than 350 students and there was no way one could control the number of participants. My purpose was to understand the aspirations of the youth, to share my experiences from my many national missions and to evolve approaches for the application of technology for societal transformation through a specially designed course of ten lectures for post-graduate students.

What do I mean by national mission? I am referring to

the space launch vehicle, SLV-3, the IGMDP (Integrated Guided Missile Development Programme), the 1998 nuclear tests, and the India 2020 report prepared by TIFAC (Technology Information, Forecasting and Assessment Council). All in all, these had a measurable impact on development and setting the growth trajectory of the nation. The objective of the SLV-3 programme was to launch a satellite indigenously for placing the 40 kg Rohini satellite in near-earth orbit. The satellite was intended for making ionospheric measurements. The IGMDP was intended to fulfil the need for force multiplier missile systems for national security, both tactical and strategic. The Agni V missile is its latest success. The nuclear tests were held on 11 and 13 May 1998. With these, India became a nuclear weapon state. TIFAC resulted in generating the road map for India to transform it into an economically developed nation by 2020.

It was my ninth lecture, entitled 'Vision to Mission', and it included several case studies. When I finished, I had to answer numerous questions and my class extended from a one-hour teaching session to two hours. After the lecture, I returned to my office, as on any other day, and had lunch with a group of research students. Prasangam, the cook, served us delicious food with a lot of smiles. After lunch, I prepared for my next class, and in the evening, I returned to my rooms.

As I was walking back, Prof. A. Kalanidhi, the vice chancellor of Anna University, joined me. He said that my office had received many telephone calls during the day and someone was frantically trying to get in touch with me. As soon as I reached my rooms, I found the telephone was ringing. When I answered, a voice on the other end said, 'The prime minister wants to talk to you.' While I was waiting to be connected to the PM, Chandrababu Naidu, who was the chief minister of Andhra Pradesh, called me on my cellphone. He told me to expect an important call from the prime minister, adding, 'Please do not say no.'

While I was talking to Naidu, the call from Atal Bihari Vajpayee materialized. He said, 'Kalam, how is your academic life?'

'It is fantastic,' I answered.

Vajpayee continued, 'We have some very important news for you. Just now, I am coming from a special meeting attended by leaders of all the coalition parties. We have decided unanimously that the nation needs you as its Rashtrapati. I have to announce this tonight. I would like to have your concurrence. I need only a "Yes", not a "No".' Vajpayee, I might mention, was heading the National Democratic Alliance (NDA), a coalition of almost two dozen parties, and it was not always easy getting unanimity.

I hadn't even had time to sit down after entering the room. Different images of the future appeared before me. One was that of being always surrounded by students and teachers. In the other, I was addressing Parliament with a vision for the nation. A decision matrix was evolving in my mind. I said, 'Vajpayeeji (as I normally addressed him), can you give me two hours' time to decide? It is also necessary that there be a consensus among all political parties on my nomination as presidential candidate.'

Vajpayee said, 'After you agree, we will work for a consensus.'

Over the next two hours, I must have made thirty telephone calls to my close friends. Among them were people in academia and friends in the civil services and in politics too. One view that came across was that I was enjoying an academic life, which is my passion and love, and I shouldn't disturb it. The second view was that this was an opportunity to put forth the India 2020 vision in front of the nation and Parliament, and that I must jump at it. Exactly after two hours, I was connected to the prime minister. I said, 'Vajpayeeji, I consider this to be a very important mission and I would like to be an all-party candidate.'

He said, 'Yes, we will work for it, thank you.'

The news travelled very fast indeed. Within 15 minutes, the news of my choice as presidential candidate was known throughout the country. Immediately, I was bombarded with an unmanageable number of telephone calls, my security was intensified and a large number of visitors gathered in my room.

The same day, Vajpayee consulted with Mrs Sonia Gandhi, the opposition leader, about the choice of candidate. When Mrs Gandhi asked whether the NDA's choice was final, the prime minister responded in the affirmative. After due consultation with her party members and coalition partners, Mrs Gandhi announced the support of the Indian National Congress (INC) to my candidature on 17 June 2002. I would have loved to get the support of the Left parties also but they decided to nominate their own candidate. As soon as I agreed to be a candidate for the presidency, a huge number of write-ups began to appear about me. Many questions were raised by the media. In essence, they were asking, how could a non-political person, particularly a scientist, become president of the nation?

~

On 18 June, at my first press conference after filing the nomination papers for my candidacy as president, journalists asked many questions regarding the Gujarat issue (the state had been racked by riots and there were concerns about how these were handled), Ayodhya (the Ram Janambhoomi issue was always in the news), the nuclear tests and about my plans in Rashtrapati Bhavan. I mentioned that India needed an educated political class with compassion as the cornerstone of decision making. On the Ayodhya issue, I mentioned that what was needed was education, economic development and respect for human beings. With economic development, societal differences would also reduce. I also pledged that I would maintain simplicity amidst the pomp and glory of Rashtrapati Bhavan. As president, on any complex issue, I would consult the country's leading constitutional experts. Decisions on issues such as President's Rule would be made on the basis of what people needed, rather than on what a few people wanted.

When I returned from Chennai to my flat in Asiad Village in Delhi on 10 July the preparations were in full swing. Pramod Mahajan of the Bharatiya Janata Party was my election agent. I set up a camp office at the flat. It was not a large flat but it had a certain flexibility. I set up a visitors' room, the conference hall was made functional, and later even an electronic camp office was set up. All data from then on was transmitted electronically. A letter was drafted for MPs – Lok Sabha as well as Rajya Sabha, so close to 800 in all – giving them my vision as president and asking them to vote for me. This was based on Mahajan's suggestion that I could send the letters without personally meeting the members of the electoral college from each state. As it turned out, I was declared elected on 18 July with a handsome margin.

There were appointments with visitors, of whom there was a stream all through the day, and interviews with media besides my own correspondence and travel. I enjoyed interacting with children and when there was time I would listen to their responses on various issues. Flat No. 833 in Asiad Village became a beehive of activity. Just drawing up the guest list for the swearing-in ceremony on 25 July was an exercise in itself. The Central Hall of Parliament can only accommodate 1,000 people. Aside from the MPs, office-bearers of the two Houses, bureaucrats from the home and other ministries, and guests of the outgoing president, K.R. Narayanan, there would be room only for a 100 guests. This we expanded to 150 or so. Who all would be in this 150 posed a problem. Family guests alone numbered thirty-seven. My old physics teacher, Prof. Chinnadurai, was there, as was Prof. K.V. Pandalai of the Madras Institute of Technology, Pakshi Venkatasubramaniam Sastrigal, chief priest of the Rameswaram temple, Imam Nurul Khuda, of the Rameswaram mosque, Rev. A.G. Leonard, priest of the Rameswaram church, and the famous eye specialist, Dr G. Venkataswamy, who started the Aravind

Eye Institute. Also among the guests was the dancer Sonal Mansingh, as were industrialists, journalists, personal friends. In the guest list, uniquely, there were 100 children from all the states of the country, for whom there was a separate enclosure. They were put under the care of a senior aide. It was a hot day but everybody came formally dressed to attend the ceremony in the historic Central Hall.

The innocence filled with wisdom of the simple people of my land always gives me the confidence that my country will lead the world to peace and prosperity.

3

SEVEN TURNING POINTS OF MY LIFE

You become the captain of the problems,
Defeat the problem and succeed.

I love teaching and research, as I never tire of repeating. Academic life is at the core of my thought, my innovation. Interaction with youth and their teachers is food for my inner self. I took a conscious decision to return to the academic and research area.

I have just described the sudden turn of events that led me to accept the presidency of the country, although I had prepared myself for a full-fledged academic career. That brings back to my memory six other events that changed the course of my life. One could add to these my re-entry into academic life in India and abroad after the presidency as a fresh transition.

~

The first turning point in my life was in 1961. I still remember, as a senior scientific assistant at the Aeronautical Development Establishment (ADE), I was the chief designer of a hovercraft. The hovercraft, called Nandi, was ready and we were demonstrating its flight to many visitors. It was a popular draw. One day, the director of the ADE, Dr Gopinath Mediratta, brought a visitor – a tall, handsome and bearded man. He asked me several questions about the machine. I was struck by the clarity of his thinking. 'Can you give me a ride in the hovercraft?' he enquired.

We took a ten-minute ride in the craft, which, in keeping with its name, hovered a few centimetres above the ground. I was piloting the vehicle, to the surprise of the visitor. He asked me a few questions about myself, thanked me for the ride and departed. But not before introducing himself – he was Prof. M.G.K. Menon, director of the Tata Institute of Fundamental Research. A week later, I received a call from the Indian Committee for Space Research (ICSR, which became the Indian Space Research Organization, ISRO) to attend an interview for the post of rocket engineer.

When I went to Bombay to attend the interview, I was surprised to find Prof. Vikram Sarabhai, who was chairman of the ICSR, along with Prof. Menon and Saraf, deputy secretary of the AEC (Atomic Energy Commission), on the interview board. I was struck by Prof. Sarabhai's warmth. He did not probe my existing knowledge and skills; rather his questions were an exploration of the possibilities I was filled with. He was looking at me as if in reference to a larger whole. The entire encounter was for me a moment of truth in which my dream was enveloped by the bigger dream of a bigger person.

The next evening, I was told about my selection. I was appointed as a rocket engineer at the newly formed ISRO in 1962. This is where the greatest event in my life came about – Prof. Satish Dhawan asking me to lead India's first satellite launch vehicle programme as its project director.

~

The second turning point was my entry into India's missile programme in 1982, following my meeting with Dr Raja Ramanna at the Defence Institute of Work Study (DIWS, now Institute of Technology Management) in Mussoorie, which is an institution that trains Services officers in defence systems management, a vast area which requires some expertise. As I had been project director of the SLV-3 programme, I was asked to give a series of lectures at DIWS. I made a presentation on how the first Indian satellite launch vehicle put Rohini into orbit. Dr Ramanna gave a lecture on how he succeeded with India's first nuclear test in 1974.

After our lectures, both of us travelled to Dehra Dun,

where we had tea with a group of scientists. While we were at Dehra Dun, Dr Ramanna offered me a position as the director of the Defence Research and Development Laboratory (DRDL) in Hyderabad. The DRDL is the mother laboratory for the development of missile systems, and comes under the Defence Research and Development Organization (DRDO). I immediately accepted the offer since I had always wanted space rocket technology to be applied in missile technology. But, my next mission was to persuade my chief, Prof. Dhawan, the ISRO chairman.

Many months went by and many letters were exchanged between ISRO and DRDO and meetings were held in the Secretariat of Defence Organizations and the Department of Space to initiate a mutually convenient course of action. Dr V.S. Arunachalam, scientific adviser to the defence minister, who was then R. Venkataraman, facilitated the discussion between the minister and Prof. Dhawan. Based on these discussions, a decision was taken to appoint me as director, DRDL, in February 1982.

~

In July 1992, I took over as the scientific adviser to the defence minister and secretary, Department of Defence Research and Development, from Dr Arunachalam. This was the third turning point in my life. In 1993, I was invited by Dr Chenna Reddy, then the governor of Tamil Nadu, to become the vice chancellor of Madras University. I requested the government to approve my appointment at the university, which I intended to pursue after I attained the age of sixty-two. However, the prime minister, P.V. Narasimha Rao, who was also defence minister, said that I must continue as scientific adviser as I was engaged in a number of important national programmes. I might add here that I worked with Narasimha Rao over many years. I found Rao very perceptive on defence issues, particularly on the question of building indigenous defence capability. He had a long-term vision of building robust systems for defence application. So I continued as scientific adviser to the defence minister till I was about seventy years of age.

The fourth turning point was the nuclear tests in 1998. There is an interesting story behind these. Let me go back to May 1996. Elections were held that year. I had met Narasimha Rao just a few days before the announcement of the results. He said to me, 'Kalam, be ready with your team for the nuclear tests. I am going to Tirupati. You wait for my authorization to go ahead with the tests. The DRDO-DAE teams must be ready for action.'

His visit to Triupati was, of course, to seek God's blessings for a good result. However, the 1996 election result was quite different from what he had anticipated. The Congress tally came down sharply, to 136 seats. The BJP and its alliance came to power but only for two weeks, led by Vajpayee, before the third front with H.D. Deve Gowda as PM took over. However in the two weeks that the Vajpayee government was there, it tried very hard to carry through the nuclear tests.

It was 9 o'clock at night. I got a call from 7 Race Course Road requesting that I immediately meet the new prime minister and Rao, the outgoing one. Rao asked me to brief Vajpayee on the details of the nuclear programme, so that a smooth handover of this important activity to the new government could take place.

About two years later, Vajpayee returned as PM. On 15 March 1998, around midnight, I got a phone call from Vajpayee. He said he was finalizing the list of ministers and wanted to induct me into his Cabinet. I told him that I needed time to think about it. He asked me to see him the next morning at 9 a.m. So in the middle of the night, I assembled a few of my friends. We debated up to 3 a.m. whether I should join the Cabinet. The general opinion was that since I was fully involved in two missions of national importance and these were in advanced stages and nearing good results, I should not leave them and enter the political system.

The next morning I went to 7 Safdarjung Road, where the PM was staying. He received me in his drawing room and first offered me home-made sweets. I then told him, 'I and my team are busy with two important programmes. One is readying the Agni missile system and another is bringing to a close the nuclear programme through a series of tests in partnership with the DAE (Department of Atomic Energy). I feel that by involving myself full-time with these two programmes, I will be contributing more to the nation. Please permit me to continue.'

'I appreciate your feelings, go ahead, God bless you,' Vajpayee responded. Many things happened after that. The Agni missile system was readied for induction, five nuclear tests were conducted consecutively, and India became a nuclear weapon state. My declining to accept the Cabinet position enabled me to contribute to two major national programmes that gave spectacular results to the nation.

∼

The fifth turning point was towards the end of 1999, when I was appointed principal scientific adviser (PSA) to the Government of India in the rank of a Cabinet minister. My team included Dr Y.S. Rajan, Dr M.S. Vijayaraghavan, who was a specialist in electronics and information science and had worked with me in TIFAC, and H. Sheridon, my personal secretary who was my staff officer when I was scientific adviser. When I started this assignment, we had no office, but we built the office, thanks to the DRDO, particularly the untiring efforts of K.N. Rai, the chief executive, Civil Works and Estates of DRDO, and Major General R. Swaminathan, chief controller, R&D, at DRDO. The India 2020 vision had been accepted by the government, hence, the office of principal scientific adviser would be a good platform to push the action-oriented plans of that document, I felt. The vision was first presented during the Deve Gowda government. Following that, I.K. Gujral came in as prime minister, and then, in 1998, it was Vajpayee again. All three governments had pushed for implementation of the recommendations. We had an office in the Vigyan Bhavan Annexe. This is a large building with the offices of various commissions of inquiry and a few government departments. It is a quiet place. The adjoining Vigyan Bhavan, of course, is famous as a venue for large national and international conferences. The annexe is next to the vice president's residence and a good place to work away from the hustle and bustle of North and South Blocks.

As usual, travel formed a good part of my work schedule. On 30 September 2001 I had a narrow escape in a helicopter crash. The crash took place just as the helicopter was landing at the Bokaro steel plant in Jharkhand. It was a miraculous escape. As soon as I jumped out, I rushed to my pilot and co-pilot and said, 'Thank you for saving me – God bless you.' The pilots were almost in tears, but I told them these things happen, all we can do is to find out the problem and solve it. That evening I had five engagements. I had to address audiences which included officials, engineers and staff of the steel plant, and students of some of the schools of Bokaro. The news of the crash had travelled quickly. The national news channels had picked it up too. When I met the children, they seemed shaken. I shook hands with all of them and shared a hymn on courage, which cheered them. It was a simple exhortation.

COURAGE

Courage to think different,
Courage to invent,
Courage to travel on an unexplored path,
Courage to discover the impossible,
Courage to combat the problems and succeed,
are the unique qualities of youth.
As a youth of my nation,
I will work and work with courage to achieve success in all
the missions.

That same day, there was the tragic air crash in which Madhav Rao Scindia and six others – journalists, his staff and crew members – were killed. These two news reports were heard by my family members at Rameswaram and my friends throughout the country and abroad. They were all extremely anxious to know how I was. I had to speak to my brother – who was not convinced by the news reports – to assure my family that everything was all right.

When I returned to Delhi later that evening, there was an urgent message from the Prime Minister's Office, requesting that I meet Vajpayee. He received me and enquired about the accident. He was happy to see me hale and hearty. He then told me that he had discussed the India 2020 vision document with industry leaders and the Cabinet and had made an announcement in Parliament for further action on it. But there are a number of hurdles in that action, I told him. It was something I had been thinking about.

The accident resulted in two important events. One was the seeding and birth of my book *Ignited Minds*, with the aim of inspiring the youth with the spirit of I can do it, and the second was my travelling from Ranchi to Quilon to meet Amma – Mata Amritanandamayee – to get myself spiritually recharged. *Ignited Minds*, as it happened, was published just before I became president. The title became a favourite phrase of the news media and occurred quite a few times in the news reports of my taking up the presidency. The book became a phenomenal success and continues to be a perennial seller. Amma is a saintly soul immersed in social welfare, specially education and health care, and helping orphans and destitutes. I was accompanied on this visit by two friends, and I shared with them that I had decided to resign as PSA and had sent a letter to the PM. Then I met Amma without any tension. I discussed with Amma my vision of India 2020 and value-based education.

This was in November 2001, after about two years as PSA. In my letter I said I would like to return to my academic pursuits. Of course, the reason was deeper, as I felt that programmes like PURA (Providing Urban Amenities in Rural Areas) and the management of India 2020 – which I was handling – were not getting the needed priority. Where was the problem arising? As far as possible I would like to implement every goal or activity as a project with well-defined timelines, funding and responsibility. Such an environment is difficult to achieve in the overall government system when the mission objective has to be accomplished by multiple ministries and departments with their own goals and programmes. In agriculture, for example, if one sets the goal of increasing production by, say, 4 per cent every year, it would need the support of the ministries of water resources, power, fertilizers, chemicals, rural development, panchayati raj, railways (for transporting the fertilizer), and so on, and there is no clear-cut, common goal for all the contributing agencies. Secondly, the PSA's is a coordinating, advisory role with a wide sweep but no direct authority, which can be a disadvantage for mission accomplishment. This led me to take up the assignment at Anna University as professor of technology for societal transformation. This was the sixth turning point in my life.

During the last three months of my tenure as president, a question was being asked about my candidature for a second term. I had already made up my mind to go back to teaching and promoting the India 2020 vision. Suddenly, in the run-up to July, the Congress ruling party suggested some likely candidates. The opposition felt differently, the nation was buzzing with political activity and a stream of leaders from different parties came to see me, suggesting that I contest again. I received several requests from the public and eminent personalities and from the youth of the nation, both personally as well as through emails, to accept a second term. Just before the close of nominations, a team of political leaders met me and said that they would get the support of all the parties, including the ruling party, if I agreed to stand for the elections.

I told them that if most parties agreed, I would consider the possibility. The leaders came back to me and said that the ruling party did not agree to my candidature, but they insisted that I should stand for the election as they were confident of my success. Without any hesitation, I told them that if that were so, I would not stand for the election since I believed that Rashtrapati Bhavan should not be drawn into party politics. Reluctantly, the leaders agreed. A press release was issued that I would not be a candidate for the presidential elections. I took a conscious decision to go back to a career in academics and research and continue to work with passion for transforming India into an economically developed nation by the year 2020.

I have always believed that cowards never make history, history is created by people with courage and wisdom. Courage is individual, wisdom comes with experience.

4

THE INTERACTIVE
PRESIDENT

*Empowerment comes from within
Nobody else can give it, except the Almighty.*

The presidency was a challenge for me. It became a
platform to launch India 2020, which I believe can only
be achieved by the participation of all citizens including
elected representatives all the way up to Parliament,
administrators, artists and writers, and the youth of the
country. The best way to convince others of the relevance
of this mission is through face-to-face discussion, which

will also help in the assimilation of others' views and thinking.

The presidency provided me with this opportunity. I could communicate directly with people across the social spectrum, particularly the youth and the political leaders, regarding the importance of having a vision for the nation that should be translated into action.

This gave my role as president an additional purpose. In respect of the constitutional role, the president has to ensure that the every action of the government and the legislatures is in line with the spirit of the Indian Constitution. Every action that the government takes is in the name of the president of India. The Bills and ordinances passed by Parliament and the government come to the president for assent and he has to ensure that these instruments are for the larger benefit of society. He also has to see that they do not set a precedent for taking an action that is biased. I will not dwell at length on the established principles and practices of the institution of president. However, besides those set by the Constitution, tradition and precedent, I felt that the role offers much more than merely that of the titular head of government.

There is scope for action on many fronts, whether it is on the development front as a catalyst for achievement by communicating with different sections of the society; politically, as he has to personally assess the strength of the party or alliance in power, so that they do not take decisions when they do not have adequate numbers; providing sagacious advice to governors and learning about the functioning of their states; and as supreme commander of the armed forces inspire them to exemplary performance.

In addition, as head of state he is the focus of people's attention. My purpose was to make Rashtrapati Bhavan much more accessible to the people and use it for reaching out to them. It was my way of making them feel a part of the growth and prosperity of the nation and give them a stake in its governance. Thus, from being president I went to being part of people's lives, and the institution became a much more interactive one.

One of the first things I did at Rashtrapati Bhavan was to initiate e-governance. There were computers in use but I felt that the process needed to be taken much further. We implemented a system whereby all the files, documents, and letters which arrived at the President's Secretariat would first get digitized and bar coded. The paper files would then be archived. From then on the file moved only electronically to various officers, directors, secretaries to the government, and to the president, according to the importance of the file.

My dream was to have a system whereby Rashtrapati Bhavan was connected to the Prime Minister's Office, governors' offices and ministries over a secured messaging network with digital signature thus enabling G2G e-governance operations. We had tested the system and it was ready for implementation. One day I hope my dream comes true. When we implemented e-governance across nine sections of the President's Secretariat, we checked if it had helped effectiveness. Normally, when the petitions from the citizens reached the Public-1 Section, for twenty petitions to get a decision, it used to take seven days, but after the implementation of e-governance it took only five hours to clear forty petitions. I hope one can see such systems in many more state and central government offices.

~

One of the important events in the early days of my presidency was inviting members of Parliament from the states and union territories for a series of breakfast meetings at Rashtrapati Bhavan, so that I could get first-hand knowledge about the status of development there. These meetings were held during a period of about three months in 2003 – from 11 March to 6 May. They made a lasting impression on my mind.

The objective of each of these meetings was well laid out and my team and I spent several weeks preparing for them. We conducted research on the competencies and development requirements of each state. The required information was collected from the Planning Commission, government departments – both central and state – national and international assessments of the state and other relevant documents.

The data was analysed and put in a presentable form using graphics and multimedia. At the meetings, PowerPoint presentations were made to the MPs with an emphasis on three areas: 1) the vision for a developed India; 2) the heritage of the particular states or union territory; and 3) their core competencies. The objective was to stress the point that to achieve the development of the nation, it was vital to achieve the development of each of these areas.

Hence a fourth aspect was also prepared – selected development indicators for each of them. And what an enrichment I got by way of preparation and by the contributions of the members of Parliament, who hailed from all parties. Meeting them helped me to understand the richness of the diverse parts of the country.

The first meeting was of parliamentarians from Bihar. I was encouraged by the enthusiasm of the members for the content of the presentation, which covered the national development profile in relation to that of Bihar, the state's core competencies and how to take the state to a developed status. The parliamentarians felt that the meeting was too short. While we increased the breakfast meeting time from 60 to 90 minutes, we had the pleasant experience that even after the meeting concluded, and after all the question-and-answer sessions, many members continued to show an interest in the presentation about their state. The meetings were put on record in a document as well.

Personally, I relished every moment of these meetings. They were a real education for me on the needs of each region. The preparations were complemented by field-level inputs from the MPs. Many of the members also told me that such comprehensive preparation was useful for them. As a matter of fact, these details and discussions continued to be a major communication bond between the MPs and myself throughout my presidency and beyond. Even now, when I meet them, development becomes a basis for conversation and discussion.

The evolution of India 2020 with inputs from many experts led me to focus on different aspects of societal transformation. The details of the states as discussed in the breakfast meetings gave me further assurance on the path to be followed for progress. The MPs gave me many useful ideas. I spoke at least nine times on the 2020 India vision in Parliament and addressed twelve state assemblies on the path to prosperity for a particular state. The type of questions and suggestions I received at the breakfast meetings paved the way to incorporate possible requirements for the state's development such as waterways, employment generation, activating public health centres, improving the connectivity of rural areas and enriching the education system in my database. This database, consisting of what I had presented to the MPs, became a reference tool to illustrate how India 2020 can be achieved when I addressed the national and state chambers of commerce and industry, management associations and technical institutions. Later, as a logical process, the ten pillars of development were evolved as a part of the vision. Today I address professionals, business leaders and researchers on how they can contribute with innovative ideas to achieve these ten pillars.

These are as follows:

1) A nation where the rural and urban divide has reduced to a thin line.
2) A nation where there is equitable distribution and adequate access to energy and quality water.
3) A nation where agriculture, industry and the service sector work together in symphony.
4) A nation where education with value system is not denied to any meritorious candidates because of societal or economic discrimination.

5) A nation which is the best destination for the most talented scholars, scientists, and investors.

6) A nation where the best of health care is available to all.

7) A nation where the governance is responsive, transparent and corruption free.

8) A nation where poverty has been totally eradicated, illiteracy removed and crimes against women and children are absent and none in the society feels alienated.

9) A nation that is prosperous, healthy, secure, peaceful and happy and follows a sustainable growth path.

10) A nation that is one of the best places to live in and is proud of its leadership.

The breakfast meetings also brought out how the leaders of the country could discuss development in a non-partisan manner. Rashtrapati Bhavan is indeed the only place where party differences disappear and the nation was seen as an integrated whole by every member of Parliament.

Apart from my meetings with MPs in Rashtrapati Bhavan, I had the opportunity to address the two Houses more than ten times.

The addresses are solemn occasions and I was heard in pindrop silence each time in the overflowing Central Hall. I had two types of interactions with Parliament. One was fully government-driven, for example the five budget speeches I gave, and the other was driven by my thoughts and ideas. Even in the government presentations, I would include certain thoughts that I wanted to discuss. Both Vajpayee and Dr Singh included my suggestions.

I used this forum to impress upon the parliamentarians their roles and responsibilities towards the nation. While addressing the parliamentarians in 2007 during a commemorative function to celebrate the 150th anniversary of our independence movement, I conveyed a message that brings out the responsibilities of MPs to their respective constituencies, to their state and to the nation. I said: 'Our movement to true freedom and independence is still incomplete; our story is still unfolding ... The time has now arrived for Parliament and legislative assemblies to emerge with a new vision and leadership to make our nation not only enlightened, united, harmonious, rich and prosperous, but above all, a safe nation, invulnerable forever to invasion and infiltration across its borders ...

The national leadership has to radiate confidence in our people and boldly emerge by formulating and implementing new national missions, targeting specific time-bound goals. India can be rightly proud of its many achievements in the economic, social and political fields over the past sixty years. But we cannot afford to rest content with past achievements and ignore recent developments that call for a change in technology, industry and agriculture. Many challenges need to be responded to: the emergence of multiparty coalitions as a regular form of government that need to rapidly evolve as a stable, two-party system; the need to strengthen internal security to cope with global terrorism and new forms of internal law and order problems; the widening of economic disparities during a period of high growth in the absence of a comprehensive National Prosperity Index in place of GDP alone; the rapid depletion of global fossil fuel reserves to be tackled by an energy independence programme; and increasing threats to our territorial security by the development of new forms of warfare . . .

I also said: When I see you, honourable members of Parliament, particularly young members, I see in you the eternal spirit of Mahatma Gandhi, Dr Rajendra Prasad, Pandit Jawaharlal Nehru, Sardar Patel, Subhash Chandra Bose, Dr Ambedkar, Abul Kalam Azad, Rajaji and many great visionary leaders of our nation. Can you also become visionary leaders, putting the nation above yourself? Can you become one of the great ones of India? Yes, you can. You can, if you enliven the Parliament with leadership for the great mission of transforming India into an economically prosperous, happy, strong and safe nation before 2020. For that to happen, honourable members, you have to have a big aim and work for the nation in the Parliament and outside. History will remember you for launching a great, bold and swift mission for the nation, a notable departure from small and fragmented actions.

~

While I was constantly engaged in working with elected members of the state assemblies and Parliament towards realizing the vision of India 2020, it was also important for me to utilize the office of governor – another important constitutional post – to work towards the same goal. In this respect, the governors' conferences held in Rashtrapati Bhavan during 2003 and 2005 become very important.

The 2003 conference was conducted against the backdrop of Prime Minister Vajpayee's commitment to ensure that India became a developed nation by 2020, as outlined in his Red Fort address the previous year and in Parliament. At the 2005 governors' conference, Prime Minister Manmohan Singh confirmed his government's commitment to the task of leading India to the same objective.

The impressive speeches at conferences get forgotten. However I placed great value on what was said, and continue to remember it as showing a serious commitment to faster development. Vajpayee stated that every part of the administrative system must recognize the need for development and further this cause, which would enable an earlier realization of our goals. This was something I could appreciate, having seen the difficulties that arise in motivating different departments to work for a combined purpose. The participating governors took the opportunity to speak their minds in an uninhibited fashion. Overall, an environment was created in which every participant could discuss problems and their solutions.

During the 2005 conference, Dr Manmohan Singh was accompanied by all his Cabinet members for a detailed discussion on the issues of education, terrorism, disaster management and implementation of Value Added Taxation based on the agenda structured by the President's Office. Appreciating the contribution made by the governors in many areas of management development, the prime minister gave his assurance that he and his colleagues would also make every effort, guided by the inspiration provided by the president. I mention this to show how the

President's Office became a very effective platform for my pet project.

~

The court cases pending in trial courts, high courts and the Supreme Court run into astonishing numbers in India. Even allowing for new cases that keep being filed, the count runs into the millions. For those involved in litigation, there is a huge cost in time, money and suffering.

In 2005, I had an opportunity to address the All India Seminar on Judicial Reforms with Special Reference to Arrears of Court Cases, where I talked about the evolution of a National Litigation Pendency Clearance Mission. I analysed the causes of delay in delivering justice, which are: 1) an inadequate number of courts; 2) an inadequate number of judicial officers; 3) the judicial officers are not fully equipped to tackle cases involving specialized knowledge; 4) the dilatory tactics followed by the litigants and their lawyers who seek frequent adjournments and delays in filing documents; and 5) the role of the administrative staff of the court.

Based on my analysis, I suggested encouraging dispute resolution through the human touch; reinforcing the Lok Adalats; creating a National Litigation Pendency Clearance Mission; ensuring alternative dispute redressal mechanisms such as arbitration; and providing fast-track courts.

I also suggested several actions with particular reference to pendency in the high courts. These included the classification of cases on the basis of an age analysis, that is, identifying cases that are redundant because the subsequent generations are not interested in pursuing them.

Primary among my recommendations was the e-judiciary initiative. As part of this, I recommended computerization of the active case files, taking into account the age analysis, which will surely reduce the number of cases that are still pending. We needed a database that would track a case from the time it was registered till it was settled with a judgement. This electronic tracking would enable easy search, retrieval, grouping, information processing, judicial record processing and disposal of the cases in a transparent manner, and make the process quicker. The complainant can find out at any time at what stage the case is, in what court a hearing will be held and when, and which issues will be dealt with by the court, enabling him to be fully prepared for the case. Apart from bringing in total transparency, the judges would also be able to track the progress of the case, the number of adjournments that had been sought, whether the grounds for these were trivial or serious and other such information that would help in the delivery of justice.

Additionally, videoconferencing could be used in a big way. This would save an enormous amount of expenditure and the unnecessary movement of police personnel accompanying those under trial.

Videoconferencing is also very useful in cases where a number of individuals are accused. The witness identification and crime reconstruction areas have also immensely benefited from the use of ICT (Information and Communication Technology).

Many countries, for example Singapore and Australia,

have also been experimenting with Internet Courts and a legal consultation service that can advise potential litigants about the legal correctness of the case that he or she wishes to pursue. In all cases, the ICT had been useful in speedy redressal of the cases as well as in avoiding fraudulent cases. This in effect would contribute to speeding up our justice delivery system.

Finally, I gave the following nine suggestions, which will enable our judicial system to administer timely justice to our citizens.

1) Judges and members of the bar should consider how to limit the number of adjournments being sought.
2) E-judiciary must be implemented in our courts.
3) Cases should be classified and grouped according to their facts and relevant laws.
4) Experts in specialized branches of law such as military law, service matters, taxation and cyber law should be appointed as judges.
5) The quality of legal education in all our universities should be improved on the pattern of law schools.
6) An exemplary penalty should be imposed for seeking undue adjournments and initiating frivolous litigation.
7) Judges of high courts and district courts may follow the suggested model for the Supreme Court and enhance the number of cases decided by them by voluntarily working extra hours on working days and Saturdays.
8) 'Multi sessions in courts' should be instituted, with staggered timings, to enhance capacity utilization with

additional manpower and an empowered management structure.

9) A National Litigation Pendency Clearance Mission should be created for a two-year operation for time-bound clearance of pending cases.

Over a period of time, I have found that our judiciary has taken note of these suggestions and has started their implementation in phases. For example, I was happy to hear of the settlement of a long-pending divorce case through videoconferencing; the husband was in India and the wife was in the United States.

India possesses one of the finest armed forces in the world, loyal, courageous and disciplined. The president is the supreme commander of the armed forces. In that capacity, I was always keen to know the environment in which our Servicemen operated, their state of readiness, their problems and challenges. As a part of this mission, I visited a number of units of the army, navy and air force. My interactions with the officers and jawans also led me to visit units stationed in difficult terrains. Hence, I specially chose to go to Kumar post on the Siachen glacier, the world's highest battleground, where our troops operate in extreme cold. I also visited the submarine operations off the coast of Visakhapatnam, and flew in a Sukhoi-30 MKI at nearly twice the speed of sound. I found these exciting experiences, and would like to share them with you.

I landed at Kumar post on Siachen Glacier on 2 April 2004. The post is located at an altitude of 7,000 metres. It was snowing and the temperature was minus 35 degrees Celsius with heavy winds. When I reached the field station, three soldiers – Naik from Karnataka, Williams from West Bengal and Salim from Uttar Pradesh – shook hands with me. The warmth of their handshakes dispelled the chill of the place. It gave me the confidence that our nation is safe in the hands of the soldiers defending it in this difficult environment. Extraordinary leadership qualities are required to generate such confidence among troops in such difficult conditions.

On 13 February 2006, I experienced a journey underwater in the naval submarine INS *Sindhurakshak*. The submarine dove to a depth of about 30 metres and started cruising. I visited the control room, where the crew explained the functioning of the submarine, showing me the manoeuvring operations and buoyancy-control mechanisms with great enthusiasm. It was a thrilling experience for me to cruise with the chief of naval staff, Admiral Arun Prakash, and the young sailors and officers. During the review, I was shown the underwater communication, target identification and launch systems. This was followed by the firing of a torpedo to simulate an attack to show the combat capability of our underwater force. The torpedo showed remarkable homing ability. I realized the complexities involved in underwater warfare.

I met the ninety officers and sailors in the vessel. Each was busy in his job. It is not an easy one but they feel proud of their challenging mission. I was given a delicious vegetarian lunch and shown a presentation on the navy's submarine plans for the next thirty years. After three hours underwater, we surfaced and returned to shore. It was in all ways a memorable journey.

∾

On 8 June 2006, I flew a sortie in a Sukhoi-30 fighter aircraft. The previous night, Wing Commander Ajay Rathore gave me lessons on how to fly. He taught me how to pilot the aircraft as well as handle the weapons control system. It was something I had wanted to do since 1958, when I became an engineer. After we were strapped in, the Sukhoi took off and soared to a height of 7,500 metres – 25,000 feet – flying at a speed of over 1,200 kilometres per hour. Wing Commander Rathore suggested a few turns and other manoeuvres. Flying a fighter aircraft can be an intensive experience and I experienced a gravitational force of about three Gs, of course with a G-suit strapped on to protect against a blackout. During the sortie I tried to understand the various systems that were developed by Indian scientists and integrated into this aircraft. I was very happy to see the indigenously built mission computers, radar warning receivers, display processors and other equipment. I was shown how to locate a target in the air and on the ground with the help of synthetic aperture radar. The flight lasted for over thirty-six minutes. I felt it was the fulfilment of a long-cherished dream.

I had opportunities too to interact with members of our paramilitary forces, central and state police personnel and internal security forces. Their dedication and valour left a deep imprint on my mind.

As president I had the opportunity to meet the entire cross-section of our society. I used this interaction to understand people, their aspirations and challenges. Equally important I could also bring people together for a common national mission.

5

WHAT CAN I GIVE TO THE NATION?

Vision elevates the nation

What can I give to the nation? Honour and respect among other countries. Putting a smile on the faces of my one billion countrymen and women. This can only be achieved through economic development and education. Education is paramount for achieving dignity. Inculcating the habit of giving will help us draw our countrymen into the mainstream of development.

The president of India is privileged to address the nation

on the eve of Independence Day and Republic Day. He uses the two occasions to apprise the country about the developments that have taken place in the period and the challenges that it faces.

The address is in English followed by Hindi. However, in a departure, in every address I started to give the greetings at the beginning and a summary of the speech in Hindi.

My knowledge of Hindi when I became President was very rudimentary. However, I felt this small bit in Hindi at the outset would at least help convey the flavour of the speech to a larger audience.

There was always a theme to the Republic Day speech. Preparation for the speech normally began well in advance. We would generate a theme, then we would seek information from multiple departments and also try and get the international picture on the subject. We would send a questionnaire to experts. Then we would collate the information. The speech would go into numerous drafts. It was not unusual for there to be ten or more drafts. The R-Day speech in 2004, for instance, had as its theme smiles on a billion faces and went through ten drafts. The focus was on values. On 14 August 2005, the theme was energy independence. The speech went through fifteen drafts. One of the highest number of drafts was, of course, for my speech to the European Parliament on 25 April 2007. This went through thirty-one drafts.

I gave ten national addresses during my tenure. The subjects of these addresses were of immense importance. They included translating vision to mission. There were also subjects like what should we be remembered for;

education for dignity of human life; an action plan for employment generation; energy independence; one billion people: one vision; national awakening; and what can I give to my nation. All these topics originated from the common idea of transforming India into a developed nation. This message had spread to citizens and professionals, leading to debates and action in their own domain. For example, as a part of employment generation, when I talked about plantation of Jatropha *curcas* in the country, a large number of states took this up as a mission and today lakhs of hectares are devoted to the plant. In addition, our experts in jatropha cultivation have enabled countries in Africa to develop plantations there with the help of our farmers, so that they can use the plant for biofuel production. Jatropha can be grown on wasteland too. Once planted it has a life of fifty years and every year it yields fruit whose seed yields an oil which can be mixed with diesel.

In the field of education, thoughts on instituting different types of student evaluations, without the threatening environment of a final examination, emerged. The Central Board of Secondary Education has introduced a grade system instead of the absolute marking system to prevent students from getting overanxious about marks, which has led to healthy competition.

On the issue of energy independence, I had suggested the creation of 55,000 MW of capacity through solar energy power plants to help the nation achieve this goal by 2030. India's energy scenario needs an integrated look. India is able to meet only 80 per cent of its coal requirements and while power demand is going up by over 5 per cent per annum, coal production increases barely by 1 per cent. In many states around the country, there are power cuts for as many as eight hours a day. Hence the development of alternative power resources becomes mandatory.

Also for maintaining the environment, we have to reduce our dependence on power plants based on coal, oil and gas. The emphasis has to be on generating clean power though the solar, wind, nuclear and hydro route. The government has announced a solar mission with a proposed generating capacity of 20,000 MW by 2020. There are other issues connected to increasing generation by solar power. For instance, extensive research is required for enhancing the present photovoltaic cell efficiency of 15 per cent to at least 50 per cent by the choice of suitable substrates. Also development work is required for using the solar power route during the day and biofuel during the night so that energy is available continuously. In Gujarat, a collaboration with the private sector has resulted in a 600 MW capacity plant for solar power. Three million units are being generated every day and bought by the state government at Rs 15 a unit.

Today, the state governments and central government have a single vision of transforming India into an economically developed nation, which has percolated down to all citizens across the length and breadth of the country.

Through all these examples, one can see that the president is fully empowered to communicate directly with the citizens and make an impact that is beneficial to the nation.

Alongside my addresses to the nation were the speeches I delivered to parliamentarians.

My address on the occasion of conferment of outstanding parliamentarian awards for the years 1999, 2000, 2001 and 2002 on 21 March 2005 made some important points.

I said: Freedom and democracy have all along been an integral part of India's culture. In fact, its history can be traced back to the very ancient period when *Sabha* and *Samiti* were two highly respected institutions in our village republics which performed functions similar to those of the popular representative bodies of today. Our choice of a democratic political system on achieving Independence was therefore an automatic continuation of the ethos that had always been there in India's culture.

We have been proud of the unparalleled distinction of India being the world's largest parliamentary democracy, one that is multi-religious, multi-language and multi-cultural. What amazes the world perhaps is the sagacity and maturity of the Indian voters who have always tried to exercise their mandate conscientiously and have proved that as envisaged in our Constitution, the people are sovereign and power flows from them. The people have a right to live in a developed India. In that context, developmental politics becomes important.

Politics has two dimensions. One is the familiar world of political parties as we know it that was essential during the time of the independence movement. However, what is needed for India today? With 260 million people living below the poverty line and an illiteracy rate of 34 per cent, and more than 36 million employment seekers, our mission has to be to make India a developed nation that is free from poverty, illiteracy and unemployment. This situation necessitates developmental politics.

I would like to visualize a situation in which the political parties perform in an environment of developmental politics in our country, competing with each other in putting forth their political vision through their manifesto. It goes like this – let me narrate some sample scenarios:

1) Suppose Party A says, within fifteen years, we will lead India into becoming a developed nation and also give a development growth plan for every five years and execute it. Party B says, we will lead India to being a developed nation within twelve years through a clear-cut action plan. Party C may unveil a new strategy for national development with different indicators and excel in ideas related to our role in the global arena. It might give a road map to ensure that India becomes a permanent member of the United Nations Security Council within a period of X years.

2) In my scenario two, Party A says, we will create a nation where there is no unemployment. They suggest achieving this through a mechanism of generating more employment providers rather than employment seekers. Party B will say we will provide an environment and mechanism where no cases are pending in the courts and ensure that law and order problems are minimized and people live in a harmonious environment. Party C says that no Indian will go to sleep hungry. It has a vision to make sure that all the

nations look up to India to provide the intellectual leadership to make the world a peaceful, stable and beautiful place to live in. World peace will be India's target.

3) In scenario three, Party A will say, we will ensure that all our border conflicts between neighbouring countries are resolved within a period of ten years. Party B will say, we will resolve all the border conflicts and create a harmonious relationship among the neighbouring countries within a period of five years. Party C might say that because of its initiatives, border trade will become borderless. Commerce brings prosperity and prosperity brings peace.

When the opportunity is given by the people to a particular party to implement its development plans and these become a reality with the support of all the members, the country and the people will be blessed by the noble act of the parliamentarians. Democracy provides an opportunity to everyone to prove to himself or herself how better he or she can perform in realizing the vision of the nation.

The need to wipe out poverty totally, the need to provide opportunities for all our people in a fiercely competitive and knowledge-based world and the need to provide security to the people and nation in the complex world of today, these multiple needs would lead to the necessity of our graduating from the 'political' politics that we know to developmental politics.

There are many national issues which have to be pursued by Parliament beyond party ideologies. These include the march towards becoming a developed nation, providing safe water, uninterrupted electricity, health care and shelter to every citizen of the country, the plans for communication and computer penetration, and national security. The consensus arrived at through discussion and debate towards these goals through the parliamentary process will certainly lead India towards the path of reaching developed status quickly. Hence, Parliament has to spend its energy in a healthy competitive spirit to help move the nation ahead.

The parliamentarians' role, therefore, assumes tremendous significance and it is essential that each MP lives up to the aspirations and ideals for which he or she has been elected.

Yet, as I told parliamentarians, there are some bare truths which we all know but refuse to acknowledge. I have no hesitation in talking to you about them, I said, because I am part of you; I am as much part of Parliament as you all are, and I am as much concerned about the success of our parliamentary system as you all are. Our polling processes have been, of late, under severe strain. Let us be honest to ourselves. The arithmetical compulsions of incremental numbers and the alleged tradability of certain legislative seats, won perhaps through means allegedly dubious and undemocratic, have many a time created doubts in our democratic system in the public mind. When politics degrades itself to political adventurism the nation would be on the calamitous road to inevitable disaster and ruination. Let us not risk it. It is time all of us did some introspection and lived up to the expectations that were enshrined so diligently and optimistically by the founding fathers in our Constitution, so that India sustained itself and grew as a mature, healthy, vibrant, democratic nation.

People are yearning for a lifestyle change by preserving the cultural heritage, values and ethos of the Indian civilization. Parliament can bring the smiles on their faces, by enacting appropriate policies, laws and facilitating societal transformation. We have been working with policies and procedures which are mostly based on mistrust. As a result, motivation and empowerment are dampened and suppressed, whereas the Indian people have shown enormous achievement when provided an environment of trust and working space.

Parliament needs to mount a mission to identify and scrap the complex old laws and administrative procedures which are hindering a growth-oriented economy. This will give scope and a hope to a large section of the people who are honest to flower and flourish. India must move to a trust-based system and only the members of this great Parliament can bring about this change, I urged them.

In order to succeed in our mission, the five key areas where India has a core competence for integrated action are: 1) Agriculture and food processing; 2) Education and health care; 3) Infrastructure: Reliable and quality electric power, good roads, and other infrastructure for all parts of the country; 4) Information and communication technology and; 5) Self-reliance in critical technologies.

These five areas are closely inter-related and if developed in a coordinated way, will lead to food, economic and national security. One of the major missions within these five areas is the development of infrastructure for bringing rural prosperity through Providing Urban Amenities in Rural Areas (PURA) by creating three connectivities, namely physical, electronic, and knowledge, leading to economic connectivity. The number of PURA clusters for the whole country is estimated to be 7,000.

While we are happy that our economy is in an ascending phase and our GDP has been growing at as high as 9 per cent per annum, it is evident that the economic growth is not fully reflected in the quality of life of a large number of people, particularly in rural areas and even in urban areas. Hence, we have evolved what is called a National Prosperity Index (NPI), which is a summation of (a) annual growth rate of GDP; (b) improvement in quality of life of the people, particularly those living below the poverty line; and (c) the adoption of a value system derived from our civilizational heritage in every walk of life which is unique to India. That is NPI=a+b+c. Particularly, 'b' is a function of availability of housing, good water, nutrition, proper sanitation, quality education, quality health care and employment potential, and 'c' is a function of promoting the joint family system, creation of a spirit of working together, leading a righteous way of life, removing social inequities, and above all promoting a conflict-free, harmonious society. This will be indicated by peace in families and communities, reduction in corruption index, reduction in court cases, elimination of violence against children and women, and the absence of communal tensions. There should be progressive reduction in the number of people living below the poverty line leading to this number becoming near zero by 2020. All our efforts at improving the national economic performance should be guided by the National Prosperity Index of the nation at any point of time.

How shall we realize this vision? What are the immediate steps that we need to take to realize this vision?

My interaction with many of you and my understanding of the various central and state programmes, the initiatives of private and non-governmental organizations as well as the overwhelming desire of citizens to participate in national development gives me the confidence that our society is ready to work for these missions. May I suggest that you all work together to evolve two major initiatives:

1) To formulate an Energy Independence Bill: A three-dimensional approach towards energy which helps maintain a clean environment.

2) Vision 2020: Adopt a resolution that India will be transformed into a safe, prosperous, happy and economically developed nation before the year 2020 using National Prosperity Index (NPI) as a measure.

You will agree with me on the importance of making these Bills a reality in a time-bound manner.

These are issues that I consider so important that I address them at some length later in the book as well.

~

I had a unique experience in Rashtrapati Bhavan. Whenever I asked for any data or information about a particular state or institution from a ministry or department of the government, the Planning Commission or the state government itself, accurate and latest information flowed

A.P.J. Abdul Kalam in The Study, the official workplace of the president.

The president giving a national address. The addresses were all focused on a theme and intensively researched.

Kalam with a young boy at Adarsh Trust, at Kureekad, Ernakulam, in 2005.

Kalam at Shishu Chetna, a rural school in Uttarakhand.

Sharing the aspirations of the youth.

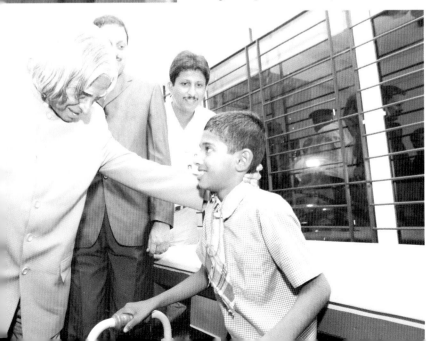

Kalam appreciating the art of a young student.

A crowd waits for the president to pass by. Kalam enjoyed unusual popularity as president.

The simplicity, warmth and astounding greenery of the North-East has always appealed to Kalam; here in Arunachal Pradesh.

Kalam giving away
the degree during a
convocation in Nagaland
University, in 2007.

An audience of
academics at one of his
lectures.

With folk dancers in Bihar, and trying his hand at a drum.

Kalam trying out a traditional farmer's hat in
Saraikela village in Jharkhand.

Relaxing with Carnatic music.

from the concerned agency without the need for sending any reminder from the President's Secretariat. This access to information was immensely useful to me for preparing my addresses to the nation, Parliament and assemblies of different states, public and private sector establishments and universities. It was an enormously useful facility that was not earlier used in the same way.

Another core competence we had built in Rashtrapati Bhavan was a virtual conference and virtual meeting facility which enabled us to have brainstorming sessions with experts from different organizations located in distant areas. During my tenure in Rashtrapati Bhavan, I had addressed twelve state assemblies and presented the missions for the prosperity of the states. The data collection, analysis, synthesis, expert inputs, brainstorming sessions leading to the preparation of missions for prosperity usually took over fifteen days to a month. Virtual conferences for this preparation were normally conducted from the Rashtrapati Bhavan multimedia facility from 8 p.m. to midnight, when the experts were generally available for consultation. The states which were covered are: Jammu and Kashmir, Himachal Pradesh, Bihar, Madhya Pradesh, Goa, Karnataka, Kerala, Andhra Pradesh, Mizoram, Meghalaya, Sikkim and Puducherry.

The criteria for selecting the missions for prosperity of the state started with the study of its socio-economic profile such as per capita income, literacy level, population below poverty line, unemployment level, infant mortality level rate, maternal mortality rate and the core competency of the state in the agriculture, industry and services sectors. For example, the missions identified for Bihar were 1) agriculture and value addition to farm produce; 2) education and entrepreneurship; 3) human resources; 4) Nalanda International University; 5) health care mission; 6) flood water management; 7) tourism; 8) infrastructure; 9) exclusive economic zone; and 10) e-governance. Ten missions were evolved to enable Bihar to increase the per capita income from Rs 6,300 (2005-06) to Rs 35,000 by 2010 and also to create an investment friendly climate leading to large-scale employment avenues for the 10 million unemployed/underemployed as on 31 December 2005. Bihar should aim at realizing the goal of 100 per cent literacy and employment by the year 2015. The government has taken up many schemes and I am happy to find that Bihar is the fastest growing state in the country today. Also, the number of people going out of the state to find work has considerably reduced which clearly brings out that large-scale value-added employment generation has taken place in Bihar.

There was good participation from the legislators. The presentations led to the initiation of many action-oriented programmes in the states. After the address to the assembly, I also addressed the vice chancellors of the universities of the state, and the chambers of commerce on the same theme.

In Kerala, *Malayala Manorama* translated the mission for Kerala's prosperity into Malayalam, conducted district-level workshops and sought the opinion of experts on the methods by which the missions can be implemented with success and the recommendations were sent to the legislative assembly. In other states too there was good coverage by the media and I received a lot of feedback from state organizations.

Connecting its one billion people by a common thread of culture and values is my dream. Our great epics remind us of our glorious past and contain the hope for a beautiful future.

6

LEARNING FROM OTHERS

May I be a protector for those without one,
A guide for all travellers on the way;
May I be a bridge, a boat and a ship
For all who wish to cross (the water)

—Acharya Shantideva,
an 8th century Buddhist Master

I have always been fascinated by the way minds come together to accomplish progress. It is not an easy process, which is why difference of views is often cited as a reason for shortfall in achievement. In the process of rocket and missile development, which involved a lot of teamwork, I began to closely observe the thinking processes of people and learn from them. The collaborative process of formulating the India 2020 vision further intensified this habit. As president and after I have been fortunate to have the benefit of ideas, opinions and criticisms of people with experience and the not-so-experienced. All shades of opinion and queries add to the enrichment of knowledge leading to human progress. I intend to narrate a few incidents that personally influenced me as a sample of thousands of interactions.

On gifts

I have mentioned this episode often so I will give it briefly. My father, Janab Avul Pakir Jainulabdeen, taught me a great lesson when I was a young boy. It was just after India won Independence in 1947. Panchayat elections were held on Rameswaram Island and my father was elected president of the village council. He was elected not because he belonged to a particular religion or caste or because of his economic status. He was elected only on the basis of his nobility of mind and for being a good human being.

On the day my father was elected as president, a man came to our home. I was still a schoolboy and was reading aloud my lessons when I heard a knock at the door. In those days in Rameswaram, we never locked the doors. A man entered and asked me where my father was. I told him that father had gone for the evening namaz. He then said that he had brought something for my father and asked if he could leave it for him. I told him he could leave the item on the cot and I continued with my studies.

When my father returned, he saw a silver plate with gifts on the cot. He asked me who had given them and I told him that someone had come by and left them for him. He opened the gifts and found expensive clothes, a few silver cups, some fruits and some sweets. He was upset and angry at the sight of the gifts. I was the youngest child and my father really loved me and I also loved him a lot. That was the first time I saw him so angry and also the first time I received a good beating from him. I was frightened and started weeping. Later, my father explained his reaction and advised me never to receive any gift without his permission. He quoted a Hadith which says, 'When the Almighty appoints a person to a position, He takes care of his provision. If a person takes anything beyond that, it is an illegal gain.'

Then he told me that accepting gifts is not a good habit. A gift is always accompanied by some purpose and therefore it is a dangerous thing. It is like touching a snake and getting its poison in return. This lesson stands out in my mind even now when I am in my eighties. The incident remains deeply embedded in my mind and has shaped my value system. Even now, when any person appears before me with a gift, my body and mind shudder.

Later in life, I studied the *Manu Smriti*, or the Laws of Manu – regarded as a foundational work of Hindu thought, which states that by accepting gifts, the divine light in a person gets extinguished. Manu warns every individual against accepting gifts for the reason that it places the acceptor under an obligation to the giver and ultimately results in making a person commit immoral or illegal acts.

A nurtured value system

One day some months ago, my elder brother who was ninety-five years old then, called me on phone from Rameswaram. He started the conversation by narrating the visit of one of my Indian friends from the United States. During the discussion, my friend asked my brother, How old is your house? He said, the house was built by our father more than a century ago. My younger brother and my earning grandchildren have now come out with a proposal to build a new house in the same place after demolishing this one. My friend said he would not want to see such a historical place being demolished. He was willing to make an arrangement through a trust to transform the house into a museum and library, while alternative accommodation was worked out for my brother and his family. My brother was calling me to say he was against the friend's proposal. 'I would like to live in the house where I have grown and lived for ninety-five years. I would like to build a new house in the same place through the earning of my kith and kin. I would not like to have any other arrangements. You thank your friend in a nice way.' It struck me, here is a man who would like to lead his life on his own terms and does not want any help, well-meant though it might be. It was a great learning for me and I saw in my brother a reflection of my father who lived to 103 years and inculcated such a tradition in us.

A Haj pilgrimage

It was a busy day. There were people to be met; decisions to be made; files to be reviewed. At that moment, my brother's grandson called from Mecca. He was managing one of the greatest projects of my life. A three-member team from my family was embarked on a memorable spiritual journey. They represented three generations of my family. My elder brother, then ninety, my brother's daughter and his grandson had departed from Chennai late in December 2005 to perform the Haj pilgrimage.

This project was very close to my heart as my brother was quite old. His faith was the main driving force for sending them on this pilgrimage. Our ambassador in Saudi Arabia came to know about their journey and called me at Rashtrapati Bhavan. He offered any help needed. I told him, I have one request, Ambassador, my brother desires to go for the Haj pilgrimage as a common citizen and without any official support. This is his personal wish. My brother insisted that he would like to go through the normal process of selection by the Haj Committee for this pilgrimage. His grandson personally submitted the application in the normal process and the committee selected them through the conventional random selection process by God's grace.

The journey was spread over fifty days covering different places and duties as they followed the pilgrimage circuit.

With him were his daughter and grandson whom I had asked to accompany my brother to support him during the pilgrimage. But my brother showed great resilience and strength to face the discomfort and uncertainties. He stayed calm allowing his grandson to take decisions and followed his instructions without any change. But unfortunately during the pilgrimage his grandson developed a high fever. My brother took charge of the situation as he has always done when the family has faced a problem. He took charge of visiting the mosque, coordinated the food requirements and summoned the doctor whenever necessary. His grandson told me that he stood by his bedside in the night praying at least for three hours, as he remembered it. Once his grandson recovered he again went into his usual mode of quiet prayer.

His grandson started explaining to me the incidents that had occurred in the last few days. After staying in tents in Mina, they proceeded to Arafat. Arafat is the place where about five million pilgrims gather. I could imagine my brother holding his hands together towards the sky and praying.

On one of the days the grandson was coming back from the upper floors of the Grand Mosque after offering prayers. The pilgrims had to walk down the stairs as the escalators had been halted to avoid accidents. But walking down the stairs was not easy with people moving close together. The grandson was forced against the wall by the jostling of the crowd. He could not breathe properly and was struggling. Suddenly he felt the pressure ease up and there was more space around him. Seeing him struggling a pilgrim from Africa with a well-built body had moved in front to protect him from the surging crowd. By the time they reached the ground floor, the pilgrim had moved away not even giving him the chance to thank him.

The second incident is even more heartening. After completing the prayers in Arafat, they were returning to Mina. All the five million pilgrims have to travel back on that 15 km stretch the same day. Their vehicle's air conditioner broke down and there was the immense heat of the desert. My brother refused to take water or food and continued to pray along the way. The vehicle inched forward every half-hour and they had been travelling for about eight hours. The driver finally suggested they walk the remaining distance to their destination, about a half-hour away on foot. My brother decided to take up the suggestion. My grandson helped him into the wheelchair despite his reluctance and started to help him along. They reached a place where they had to cross a small fissure in the road. My brother had to get down from the wheelchair and cross the fissure. Two pilgrims who saw this signalled to my brother to remain seated. Even before his grandson could say anything, they just lifted my brother with the wheelchair and placed him across the fissure. This time also they didn't wait for someone to thank them.

In a place called Muzdalifa, they had to spend the night in the open. It was a cold desert night and they slept on the ground with only a mat underneath them. As they wore only very light clothing, this offered little protection against the cold. Early in the morning there was a huge queue for the washrooms. All the people who would otherwise have fought for their turn back home were standing in patient silence. In one of the queues, a lady had been waiting for her turn for almost one hour. A young girl came up to the queue and asked the woman to allow her to go out of turn.

All the others in the queue let the woman decide. She let the young girl go. As it happened, after some time an old woman came and she too asked to be allowed to go first. This time all the onlookers thought after waiting for so long she would not allow the old lady to precede her. But to their surprise she made way for the old lady instantly. One has to remember that they did not know each other's language and relied on signs. But the episodes show how even small gestures transform our lives in big ways.

Given the opportunity, love towards our fellow human beings flows like an uninhibited river, washing away all differences, was what I gathered from the narration by my brother's daughter Nazima and grandson Gulam K. Moinudeen.

Field Marshal Sam Manekshaw

There was a call at Rashtrapati Bhavan from the Field Marshal when I was visiting Coimbatore in 2006. When I was informed of it I said, I must visit the Army Hospital in Wellington and see him. Let me recount my first meeting with him.

During the 1990s, one day I was travelling on an Indian Airlines flight and found myself next to Field Marshal S.H.F.J. 'Sam' Manekshaw. I introduced myself as the scientific adviser to RM (Raksha Mantri, that is, defence minister). When I told him this, he asked me, 'Is he a good guy?' The next question he asked me was, 'How old are you?' I said I am sixty-nine. He said, 'You are a bachcha (child)'! I never thought I would meet the field marshal as a supreme commander of the armed forces. As soon as I entered his room, he told everybody to go out. He asked me to sit close to him and took my hand and said, 'What a president you are, when I am not in power, you are honouring a soldier.' He was very happy to see me. Old as he was, and bedridden, his mind was still on maintaining the effectiveness of our armed forces. They had to be continuously strengthened, he said, because of adversaries and evolving defence technologies. He asked me an interesting question. 'Kalam, can you tell me, in another decade will all the existing weapons become meaningless and will electronic and cyber warfare take over?' This question from the field marshal was ringing in my mind and came up when I met a great spiritual leader and we discussed ridding the world of nuclear weapons. When I asked the field marshal, 'Can I do anything for you?' he said, 'I do not know, but one thing I want to tell you, the status of the field marshal of the country or the equivalent has to be unique for the nation.' This remark stayed in my mind.

As soon as I came to Delhi, I had a meeting with the prime minister for some other purpose. I told him that we must do something more in recognition of the great service rendered by Field Marshal Manekshaw for the country. That day there was a dinner for visiting dignitaries where I met the army chief and the air force chief and emphasized the need for recognizing both Field Marshal Manekshaw and Marshal of the Air Arjan Singh. Then I immediately called my secretary, P.M. Nair, to prepare a note and send it to the prime minister for necessary action with retrospective effect. The government gladly accepted the proposal to refix his pay scale consistent with his contribution to the nation. I was very happy that the recognition took place during the lifetime of Field Marshal Sam Manckshaw.

The inimitable Khushwant

It was a great experience to meet Khushwant Singh, who is now in his nineties. I have read some of his books, and have been an ardent reader of his column in the *Hindustan Times*. Many people asked me why I had specially met him. My answer was, I particularly like books and their authors. Khushwant Singh is a great and ceaseless writer, even at the age of ninety-five. He did a write-up on me in 2007 in his column. I give an abridged version which illustrates his views, and my own, on God quite interestingly, I thought.

> In a few months Abdul Kalam, the eleventh President of our Republic, will retire after serving a full term of five years. He is the third Muslim to have held the highest office: A fair record of our claim to be a secular democracy and a lesson to our neighbours.
>
> I have no idea whether he will return to scientific research, teach in some university or take sanyas. He is in his 70s. I had the privilege of spending half an hour with him. He did the honour of visiting me in my apartment: The head of state calling on a common pen-pusher speaks well of his humility.
>
> We have very little in common. He is Tamil. I know only two words of Tamil: *Venakkam* and *ai-ai-yo*. Though a scientist, Kalam is a deeply religious man. I am an agnostic and believe that science and religion cannot go together. One is based on reason, the other on faith. After talking to him and reading his writings, I found his

religious beliefs are similar to Mahatma Gandhi's. Despite my inability to accept all that Bapu stood for, I call myself a Gandhian. Kalam sees no conflict between science and religion. When I asked him if he believed in the Day of Judgement and rewards or penalties we might have to pay in life hereafter, he replied evasively, 'Heaven and hell are in the mind' . . .

So what is Kalam's concept of God? It is not Allah versus Ishwar, Khuda versus Bhagwan; He is not to be looked for in a mosque or a temple. He is not to be fought over and sought in martyrdom as protagonists of different religions do in our country. After they have shed each other's blood, comes the voice of God-like thunder:

Suddenly a sound thundered from light,
'I am none of yours! All ye hear!
Love was my mission and you spent it on hatred,
Killing my delight, stifling life.
Know ye all: Khuda and Ram
Both are one, blossoming in love.'

No rationalist can dispute Kalam's vision of divinity. Some define God as truth; others as love. Kalam's concept of godliness is compassion . . .

I quote from him because I consider it a rare honour to have had a writer like him spend so much time analysing my work and presenting my way of thinking about God, religion and what constitutes a good human being.

In giving we receive

Of course some of you may be blessed with wealth. Here I present the story of a great human being who has given freely and spread happiness in the world. I received a personal invitation which said that I must come to inaugurate the 100th year celebrations of Sree Sree Sivakumara Swamigalu at Siddaganga Math in 2007. When I reached there, I saw a mammoth gathering of lakhs of devotees to greet the seer. Also on the dais were many political and spiritual leaders. After they had all spoken, Swamiji got up without any paper in his hand and gave an extempore speech blessing his devotees. I was astonished by the scene. A 100-year-old seer, standing erect, smilingly delivering his speech, made me ask myself how he had retained his energy and enthusiasm so well. It is only because he had been giving so freely, I thought, through the creation of hundreds of educational institutions, many orphanages and feeding thousands of needy people every day. His tireless mission of service and his effort to eradicate illiteracy and discrimination through giving has uplifted many people in the region. I was moved to write:

WHAT CAN I GIVE?

O my fellow citizens,
In giving, you receive happiness,
in body and soul.
You have everything to give.
If you have knowledge, share it.
If you have resources, share them with the needy.

Use your mind and heart,
To remove the pain of the suffering,
And cheer the sad hearts.
In giving, you receive happiness.
Almighty will bless all your actions.

Interactions with PMs

In the course of my functioning as director of DRDL, scientific adviser to the defence minister, principal scientific adviser to the Cabinet and as president of India, I have had an opportunity to interact with many great personalities like Dr Satish Dhawan, Dr Raja Ramanna, Dr V.S. Arunachalam, R. Venkataraman, P.V. Narasimha Rao, H.D. Deve Gowda, I.K. Gujral, Atal Bihari Vajpayee and Dr Manmohan Singh. These associations were extremely fruitful and they left an indelible mark in my mind. I learnt from Dr Satish Dhawan who was my boss and chairman of ISRO that when you execute complex missions you always encounter challenges and problems. He used to say that you should not allow problems to become your captain, you should become the captain of the problems, and defeat them and succeed. This is a great learning for anyone engaged in a complex mission. Dr Raja Ramanna and Dr Arunachalam showed the ability to recognize the value of the individual and would work hard to get the right individual for a complex task. R. Venkataraman as defence minister could foresee the needs of our country for large force multiplier systems for the Services and took a decision to mount such programmes which are paying off with large dividends today.

Narasimha Rao was an extremely clear-headed person who had a grasp of every subject related to the development of the country. Once he was chairing a defence consultative committee when the director-general of supplies and transport, ASC (Army Supply Corps) was making a presentation about the performance of the dairy farms and their modernization plans. During the presentation, the DG mentioned that progressively they were weaning out the buffaloes and replacing them with Jersey cows. Rao was quick to realize that buffaloes are unique to our country, they can live in the tropics with cheap fodder and food and yield high-protein milk. The country cannot afford to lose this native wealth. Hence, he gave directions that this proposal should be reviewed and urgent corrective action should be taken by the army dairy farms.

On another occasion, while I was presenting the report on self-reliance in defence systems some time in 1995, Rao was quick to observe that we were making a premise that the defence expenditure should be less than 3 per cent of the GDP. He said that we should not put such a limit; we should work on what is essentially needed for building a strong defence system for the nation. The GDP may be continuously varying, and we could not have the expenditure going up and down on that account.

I remember one more example. The DRDO had to take up a follow-up programme for the Agni missile system beyond the technology demonstrator which could be inducted into the Services. Rao understood the need instantaneously and approved a Rs 800 crore programme, based on a one-page proposal, without any question and provided an opportunity to design a need-based management system for timely execution and delivery of missiles to the Services. Subsequently, the programme was approved by the finance minister, Dr Manmohan Singh, to whom it would have gone before going to the prime minister in the normal course. The file was later moved to the secretaries of the Government of India who were in the execution chain. This was an example of a top-down approach in programme conception, sanction and implementation.

Later, in 2004, I had an opportunity to work closely with Dr Singh who as prime minister has applied all his economic skills to enhance growth, which has reached as high as 9 per cent in recent years. He has brought a warm and human touch to the office of the prime minister. I could see the sense of urgency in decision making in Atal Bihari Vajpayee who gave me the task of execution of the nuclear tests as my first job as soon as he took over as prime minister in 1998. In general, I found Vajpayee was decisive in all his actions while dealing with any national problem. He was the person who made an announcement that India would work towards becoming a developed nation by 2020 from the ramparts of the Red Fort in August 2002, as I have already said. The first time India 2020 was accepted as a national programme was by H.D. Deve Gowda in 1998.

The experience of meeting good people is an education in itself. I have been fortunate to meet more than my share of such people in various phases of my life.

7

TOWARDS A COMPETITIVE NATION

National economic development is powered by competition.
Competition is powered by knowledge. Knowledge is powered by
technology and innovation.

The majority of India's population lives in the villages. And that is the real challenge for the scientific community: to use the results of technology to enrich the lives of the 750 million people who live there.

In my fifty-year career in the fields of science and technology, I have always believed that keeping ahead in these two areas is the only way for a developing nation to become a developed nation. The three major areas on which we must focus are nanotechnology, e-governance and bio-diesel. With regard to creating a favourable environment for innovation, I felt, why not make a start in Rashtrapati Bhavan itself?

Complex and new initiatives require the combined thinking of many specialists, the consideration of different opinions and a collective effort to execute missions and actions. In this regard, there were three unique events that took place in Rashtrapati Bhavan and Rashtrapati Nilayam, the presidential retreat in Secunderabad. These were a nanotechnology conference, an e-governance conference and a bio-diesel conference. In terms of potential impact on the future of the country, each of these events was very significant.

I had long been discussing with Prof. C.N.R. Rao – honorary president of the Jawaharlal Nehru Centre for Advanced Scientific Research in Bengaluru – and many other specialists in India and abroad the future directions in the research and development of nanoscience technology and its potential applications in areas like agriculture, medicine, space and energy. These discussions prompted me to host a full-day conference in Rashtrapati Bhavan. The discussions and recommendations eventually resulted in a coordinated programme with an outlay of Rs 1,000 crore. This programme led to several important advances and innovations. For example, I was delighted to learn that scientists from the Banaras Hindu University had devised a simple method to produce carbon nano-tube filters that efficiently remove micro- to nano-scale contaminants from water and heavy hydrocarbons from petroleum. The scientists and technologists of Delhi University in partnership with a private company, Dabur, have successfully developed a drug delivery system that directly targets tumour cells.

Efficient, result-oriented and transparent governance is a prerequisite for a developed India and our progress as a knowledge society. An integrated system with a decentralized set-up at the state, district, and village level is essential for this. The planning and implementation of this requires a concerted effort from the central and state governments as well as private and public sector participation. Keeping this in mind, an e-governance conference was held with the participation of the concerned agencies. We also introduced a system of e-governance in Rashtrapati Bhavan. I have addressed the judiciary, audit agencies and many other sectors on this subject. A presentation was also made to the Commonwealth meet, which was well appreciated. It is my hope that an e-governance system with smart identification cards for each citizen will make for effective services and will also contribute to our fight against extremism and terrorism.

I believe that the two key areas that will be sources of conflict in the future are water and energy. One of the governors' conferences addressed the water issue in terms of maintenance of water bodies, conservation of this resource and the networking of rivers both within states and nationally. I have been propagating energy independence from fossil fuels as the need of the hour. One key initiative in this regard is developing biofuel. To highlight this and to consider all aspects of the initiative in an integrated way we hosted a conference at Rashtrapati Nilayam. Among others, the conference was attended by farmers who have experience in this field and are also potential users. The vice chancellors of agricultural universities explained the research on different aspects like seed characteristics and irrigation needs of plants which could be used as sources of biofuel. Government officials raised issues related to allotment of non-fertile lands. Automobile designers talked about a mix of biofuel and diesel that could be used without any changes in engine design and the changes required if the percentage of biofuel used were to be higher. Business representatives talked about investments and breakeven points. I presented my concept for the use of biofuel. At the end of the conference recommendations were drawn up and circulated to the concerned parties. I am glad that a biofuel policy has now been evolved.

In addition to these three conferences, there was another technological event which germinated from Rashtrapati Bhavan.

∼

In 2006, the then chairman of ISRO briefed me on his future space plans including the Chandrayaan mission to explore the moon, which I am sure is just the first step towards further planetary explorations and manned missions. Regarding the proposed moon mission, he told me that the spacecraft would orbit the moon and transmit scientific information on the chemical, mineralogical and geological characteristics of the heavenly body. He also told me that the mission would carry a variety of scientific instruments, which ISRO was in the process of finalizing. I suggested that the mission could include a combined entry package to the moon with at least one telemetry channel, with density or pressure measurement or tone ranging. This payload would enable us to gather data directly from the moon's surface. The chairman promised to include this payload. This led to the birth of the Moon Impact Probe as a part of the Chandrayaan mission. To my delight, the probe landed on the moon's surface on 14 November 2008 exactly in the pre-determined area. I congratulated the ISRO team for this fine achievement.

These two highly technical initiatives took place at the instance of Rashtrapati Bhavan. I was very happy to be a partner in such promising ventures.

When I was studying the global innovation report for the year 2011, I found that as per the Global Innovation Index Switzerland is ranked 1, Sweden 2, Singapore 3, Hong Kong 4, and India 62. There is a relationship between the innovation index and competitiveness. While India is 62 in the index, our ranking in Global Competitiveness Index was 56 in 2010-11. If India has to graduate from 56 and become equal to the developed nations (within the top 10), it is essential that we build indigenous design capability. The present growth has been achieved by the use of technologies essentially developed elsewhere based on scientific discoveries and patents generated ten to fifteen years earlier. The latest technologies resulting from scientific advances are not available from developed countries to India at least for a decade. Hence, research is vital, particularly in basic sciences, to take up India's global competitiveness to the desired level. I give below the result of one endeavour where India developed the required technology.

∾

We crossed a milestone recently. On 19 April 2012, the tension sharpened at the launch area at Wheeler Island on the Odisha coast as the massive, 50-tonne, 17.5-metre-high Agni V missile was elevated into the vertical launch position, and the pre-launch checks began. At 8.07 a.m. the countdown began and a giant ball of fire leaped out as the missile's first stage ignited. As Agni V rose smoothly off the launch pad, scientists checked its systems audibly on the public address system, their voices calm, in contrast to the tension among the viewers. After 90 seconds, the first stage burnt out and separated. The missile was travelling at exactly the speed it should have been. Then, on schedule, the all-new composite second stage burnt out and separated.

Within minutes, the missile was in space, streaking southwards for 2,000 km until it crossed the equator. Then, it hurtled along for another 3,000 km, re-entering the atmosphere over the Tropic of Capricorn and splashing down between the southern tip of Africa and Australia. From launch to splashdown it took just 20 minutes. Indian naval vessels tracked the missile all along its course, including at the terminal stage. The missile hit the target within the pre-determined accuracy.

The IGMDP was sanctioned at a cost of nearly Rs 400 crore in 1983. This programme envisaged development, production and deployment of four missile systems namely, a surface-to-surface missile (Prithvi); a medium-range surface-to-air missile (Akash); a short-range quick reaction surface-to-air missile (Trishul); and an anti-tank missile (Nag). In addition, a technology demonstration missile (Agni) was also a part of the programme, which was intended to show the re-entry characteristics of a long-range missile. This technology was first demonstrated on the Odisha coast in May 1989. Subsequently longer ranges of Agni I, II, III and IV were demonstrated during the last two decades with increasing range capabilities. And finally the scientists and engineers of DRDO facilitated the flight testing of Agni V, which is a 5,000 km range missile. All these missiles come under the category of MTCR (Missile Technology Control Regime) and other sanctions. Hence, neither the missile system, nor the technology needed for these systems will be available for purchase for a price. The system has to be realized in a hard way only through systematic research and development.

Hence, the successful testing of this missile holds a special significance in terms of self-reliance in critical technologies and empowers the country to follow an independent foreign policy.

My friend Dr V.K. Saraswat and his team briefed me on the launch of Agni V.

Allow me a little history. I mention one conversation from 1984 and the other occurred in 1991. I was director of DRDL at Hyderabad. Prime Minister Indira Gandhi after sanctioning the IGMDP through her Cabinet in 1983 came to DRDL to review the programme the next year. While we were presenting the progress of the programme, Mrs Gandhi saw a world map in the conference hall. She asked us to stop the presentation and directed our attention to the world map. She said, 'Kalam, look at the map, look at the distances shown there. When will the laboratory launch a missile which will be capable of reaching places as far away as that to meet any contingency' (she pointed to a spot 5,000 km away from Indian territory). Of course, our DRDO scientists have now achieved the goal envisioned by this great stateswoman.

Subsequently, when Prithvi had demonstrated successful performance, the army came up with another important requirement. The army wanted to have a confirmatory test, on a land range, to validate Circular Error Probability (CEP). Our efforts to conduct the test in our desert range could not take off due to range safety and geopolitical problems. To overcome this we were looking for an uninhabited island on the eastern coast. On the hydrographic map supplied by the navy, we saw a few islands in the Bay of Bengal off Dhamra (on the Odisha coast) indicating that there was some landmass there. Our range team consisting of Dr S.K. Salwan and Dr V.K. Saraswat hired a boat from Dhamra and went in search of the island. On the map these islands were marked as 'Long Wheeler', 'Coconut Wheeler' and 'Small Wheeler'. The team carried a directional compass and proceeded on the journey. They lost their way and could not locate Wheeler Island. Fortunately, they came across a few fishing boats and asked them for the route. The fisherman did not know about Wheeler Island but they said there was an island called 'Chandrachood'. They thought that this could be the one they were looking for. They gave the direction for proceeding to Chandrachood. With their guidance the team could reach Chandrachood Island, which was later confirmed as Small Wheeler Island and had adequate width and length required for range operations.

To get to the island, we had to go through the Odisha bureaucracy. The necessity arose for a political decision from the chief minister (in 1993). At that time, Biju Patnaik, who was a powerful national leader, was the chief minister. The indications from the chief minister's office were that the island could not be parted with for several reasons. However, an appointment was arranged for meeting Patnaik to put in our request. When we reached his office, the file was in front of him. The CM said, 'Kalam, I have decided to give all the five islands at no cost to you (DRDO), but I will sign the file of approval only when you give me a promise.' He held my hand and said, 'You must make a missile that can protect us from even distant threats.' I said, 'Sir, definitely we will work for it.' I immediately informed our defence minister. The chief minister signed the file and we got Small Wheeler Island.

~

Readers, as you might be aware, ISRO successfully launched India's first Radar Imaging Satellite (RISAT-1) on 26 April 2012. The satellite was on board the Polar Satellite Launch Vehicle (PSLV-C19) and launched from the Satish Dhawan Space Centre at Sriharikota. Subsequent to the injection of the satellite into orbit, the solar panels and antenna panels of C-band Synthetic Aperture Radar of RISAT-1 were successfully deployed. Further, the satellite was successfully placed into polar sun-synchronous orbit through a series of four orbit-raising manoeuvres. High quality images, starting from Gangotri and passing through Bhopal and parts of north Karnataka were acquired and processed on 1 May 2012.

The mission illustrates some important technologies. I will mention some aspects in brief.

Unlike optical remote sensing satellites, the Synthetic Aperture Radar in RISAT-1 transmits its own radar pulses for imaging of the earth surface. This facilitates cloud penetration and imaging even without sunlight. Thus it can image an area irrespective of the weather and sunlight conditions. RISAT-1 has imaging capabilities in multiple modes and polarizations with imaging resolutions from 1 to 50 metres and swath coverage from 10 km to 223 km. Important applications of RISAT-1 include agricultural sector mapping of paddy crops during kharif season through identification, classification and acreage estimation and mapping of inundated areas during floods and cyclones as a part of disaster management, besides numerous other applications.

This is only to give a glimpse of our confidence and the range of our space activities. There are many other successes

I could elaborate upon. For instance, the test flight of the naval variant of the Light Combat Aircraft (LCA) at Bengaluru on a partially cloudy day. With the successful maiden flight of the LCA's naval variant, India joins an elite club of countries capable of designing, developing, manufacturing and testing the fourth generation carrier-borne fly-by-wire 'ski take off but arrested recovery' (Stobar) aircraft. The naval variant is the first attempt to provide a complete marine force multiplier that will give unique battle capability to the naval aviation arm of the twenty-first century Indian Navy. Its accomplishment represents success in overcoming a series of design challenges.

Information technology and communication technology have already converged leading to Information and Communication Technology. Information technology combined with biotechnology has led to bio-informatics. Similarly, photonics has emerged from the labs to converge with classical electronics and microelectronics and bring in new high-speed options in consumer products. Flexible and unbreakable displays using a thin layer of film on transparent polymers have emerged as new symbols of entertainment and media tools. Now, nanotechnology has come in. It is the field of the future that will replace microelectronics and many fields with tremendous application potential in the areas of medicine, electronics and material science.

When nanotechnology and ICT meet, integrated silicon electronics, photonics are born and it can be said that material convergence will happen. With material convergence and biotechnology linked, a new science called Intelligent Bioscience will be born which would lead to a disease-free society with longevity and high capabilities.

The convergence of science is reciprocating. Let me give an example. Recently, I was at Harvard University where I visited the laboratories of many eminent professors from the Harvard School of Engineering and Applied Sciences. I recall how Prof. Hongkun Park showed me his invention of nano needles, which can pierce and deliver content into individual targeted cells. That's how nanoparticle science is shaping the biosciences. Then I met Prof. Vinod Manoharan, who showed on the other hand how bioscience is in turn shaping nanomaterial science as well. He is using DNA material to design self-assembling particles. When a particular type of DNA is applied on a particle at the atomic level, it is able to generate a prefixed behaviour and automatic assembly. This could be our answer to self-assembly of devices and colonies in deep space without human intervention as envisioned by Dr K. Eric Drexler. Thus, within a single research building, I saw how two different sciences are shaping each other. This reciprocal contribution of sciences to one another is going to shape our future and industry needs to be ready for it. We need to bring down the barriers existing between various technological groups that inhibit research.

Lastly, globally, the demand is shifting towards development of sustainable systems which are technologically superior. This is the new dimension of the twenty-first-century knowledge society, where science, technology and environment will have to work together. Thus, the new-age model would be a four-dimensional bio-nano-info-eco-based one holding exciting possibilities.

I would like to ask you, what would you like to be remembered for? You should write it down. It could be an important contribution, whether it is an invention, an innovation or a change that you bring about in society that the nation will remember you for.

8

THE CANDLE AND
THE MOTH

The lamps are different
But the light is same.
Worldly joys you returned to the world,
You remain in my innermost soul.

The crash of the Airborne Surveillance Platform on 11 January 1999 left me devastated. It brought home a different facet of the scientific endeavour, a tragic one. My conversation with my friend Prof. Arun Tiwari brings out my feelings about this experiment that did not succeed as planned. It is also my tribute to the people who participated in it.

Arun Tiwari (AT): The essential issues of life tend to arise naturally during transitions and intense events. They can also be brought forth through introspection. They arise especially as the soul learns to penetrate and transcend its ego structure. Franz Kafka wrote in his celebrated masterpiece 'Metamorphosis' on this theme.

APJ: I can see that. The period that followed the failure of the first flight of SLV-3 and the pre-launch difficulties in Agni's first flight trial made me discover my real self in a very significant manner. But the Arakonam crash in 1999 was a devastating experience for me, also in terms of what it did to my ego structure.

AT: You have never discussed that. I could only see the tip of the iceberg of the enormous pain that you have always kept submerged in the ocean of your work. Would you like to share it?

APJ: More than the sharing aspect, I wish to express my gratitude to the eight young men who sacrificed their lives in a scientific endeavour. The nation must know about those unsung heroes. The pain their families suffered must be shared.

AT: Sir, are you talking about the Airborne Surveillance Platform (ASP) crash on 11 January 1999?

APJ: Yes. The ASP crashed into the dense forests near Arakonam.

AT: I spoke once with K. Ramchand about this incident. He was the systems engineer. He told me that the Avro aircraft, with airborne surveillance system mounted atop as a rotodome, took off around 1400 hrs, climbed up to 10,000 ft and set course towards the Chennai coast. The radar testing was carried out between the Arakonam-Chennai coastline. The target aircraft for the mission trial was an AN-32 aircraft, which took off 15 minutes before the Avro. The radar performance was checked with both sea and land clutter. The performance of the radar as reported by the onboard mission crew via VHF (very high frequency) communication was very good. After one and a half hours of flight testing, the target aircraft landed at Arakonam around 1600 hrs. Subsequently, the ASP aircraft set course from Chennai towards Arakonam and descended close to the airfield from 10,000 to 5,000 ft. When the aircraft was about five nautical miles away from the airfield at an altitude between 3,000 ft and 5,000 ft, the rotodome severed away. The aircraft became unstable and crashed killing all the eight occupants.

APJ: I was in a Defence Research Council meeting in my office in South Block when I was told about the crash. I rushed to Bangalore to be with the bereaved families. Air Chief Marshal A.Y. Tipnis was also there. It was a very difficult moment for me, seeing the young wives crying in desperation and parents standing shell-shocked. One lady thrust her infant into my lap, saying, 'Who will look after this young life?' Another lady cried. 'Why did you do this to us, Mr Kalam?'

AT: Ramchand gave me the list of the officers who lost their lives. Sqn Ldr P. Venkataraman was piloting the aircraft. P. Ilango, instrumentation engineer, and K.P. Shaju, radar system engineer, were from the Centre for Airborne Systems (CABS); D. Narasimhaswamy, radar processing scientist, and I. Jayakumar, signal processing scientist, were from the Electronics Research and Development Establishment (LRDE); and Sqn Ldr N.V. Seshu, R. Bhatnagar and S. Ravi were the other air force officers.

APJ: There were hardly any remains. For the comfort of the families, the authorities made coffins and kept them in the community hall.

AT: O my God!

APJ: In my state of profound grief, I could barely mumble a few words in the farewell speech I had to make.

AT: It reminds me of the letter Abraham Lincoln wrote to a mother of five sons who had died gloriously in the civil war.

> I feel how weak and fruitless must be any words of mine which should attempt to beguile you from the grief of a loss so overwhelming. But I cannot refrain from tendering to you the consolation that may be found in the thanks of the Republic they died to save.
>
> I pray that our Heavenly Father may assuage the anguish of your bereavement, and leave you only the cherished memory of the loved and lost, and the solemn pride that must be yours, to have laid so costly a sacrifice upon the altar of freedom.

APJ: The memory of wailing widows, immobilized parents, an innocent infant in my lap and the cremation of symbolic coffins haunts me sitting here in Rashtrapati Bhavan. Do the few around going through the motions of politics and protocol understand the pain and agony people suffer out there in the laboratories and fields?

AT: What is the message?

APJ: Don't pretend to be a candle, be a moth. Know the power hidden in serving. We seem to have got stuck with external forms of politics and mistaking them to be nation-building. It is sacrifices, toil and valour that is seldom shown or seen that truly makes a nation.

The crash of the airborne surveillance platform was one of the most tragic events in my life. I have given this conversation to show how deeply I feel about it. As also to convey that it is a long, hard journey while undertaking complex missions. But such setbacks also serve to toughen us.

9

MY VISIT TO GUJARAT

Angel is free because of his knowledge,
The beast because of his ignorance,
Between the two remains the son of man to struggle.

—Rumi

One of the pillars of development that I have thought a lot about is that we have to create a nation where poverty has been totally eradicated and illiteracy removed. Alongside, we need to evolve a society where crimes against women and children are absent and none in the society feels alienated. These thoughts were prominent in my mind during my visit to Gujarat in August 2002, which I took up as my first major task immediately after becoming president. The state had been hit by riots a few months earlier, and their impact had left thousands of lives in disarray. It was an important and sensitive task, because it took place under unique circumstances, in a politically charged atmosphere. I decided that my mission was not to look at what had happened, not to look at what was happening, but to focus on what should be done. What had happened was already a point of discussion by the judiciary and the Parliament and continues to be discussed even now.

As no president had ever visited an area under such circumstances, many questioned the necessity of my visit to the state at this juncture. At the ministry and bureaucratic level, it was suggested that I should not venture into Gujarat at that point of time. One of the main reasons was political. However, I made up my mind that I would go and preparations were in full swing at Rashtrapati Bhavan for my first visit as president.

The prime minister, Atal Bihari Vajpayee, asked me only one question, 'Do you consider going to Gujarat at this time essential?' I told the PM, 'I consider it an important duty so that I can be of some use to remove the pain, and also accelerate the relief activities, and bring about a unity of minds, which is my mission, as I stressed in my address during the swearing-in ceremony.'

Many apprehensions were expressed, among them that my visit might be boycotted by the chief minister, that I would receive a cold reception and that there would be protests from many sides. But, to my great surprise when I landed at Gandhinagar, not only the chief minister, but his entire Cabinet and a large number of legislators, officials and members of the public were present at the airport. I visited twelve areas – three relief camps and nine riot-hit locations where the losses had been high. Narendra Modi, the chief minister, was with me throughout the visit. In one way, this helped me, as wherever I went, I received petitions and complaints and as he was with me I was able to suggest to him that action be taken as quickly as possible.

I remember one scene, when I visited a relief camp. A six-year-old boy came up to me, held both my hands and said, 'Rashtrapatiji, I want my mother and father.' I was speechless. There itself, I held a quick meeting with the district collector. The chief minister also assured me that the boy's education and welfare would be taken care of by the government.

While I was in Ahmedabad and Gandhinagar, people from all sections of society wished to talk to me and express their problems and views personally. In one such gathering, nearly 2,000 citizens of Ahmedabad surrounded me. The interaction was in Gujarati and a friend of mine translated. I was asked about fifty questions and received 150 petitions.

My visit to two important places in Ahmedabad was indeed significant, particularly in the light of the riots. I called on Pramukh Swamiji Maharaj at Akshardham where he welcomed me. I discussed with His Holiness the mission of achieving unity of minds and bringing a healing touch to Gujarat, which has given to the nation great human beings like Mahatma Gandhi, Sardar Vallabhbhai Patel and Vikram Sarabhai.

I also visited Sabarmati Ashram, where I met many ashramites and saw the agony writ large on their faces, even as they mechanically carried out their normal chores. I witnessed similar sentiments at Akshardham as well. As I was wondering why, I realized that both these institutions, by virtue of their inherent love and respect of human beings and their spiritual environment, work to bring happiness, peace and progress to society and could therefore not accept a situation of inflicting avoidable pain. I say this because in our land, with its heritage of a highly evolved civilization and where great men were born and stood tall as role models for the entire world, communal riots with their attendant tragedy are an aberration that should never happen.

All through my visit only one thought occupied my mind. We have many important tasks at hand to improve the lot of people and to accelerate the process of development. Should not development be our only agenda? Any citizen following any faith has the fundamental right to live happily. No one has the right to endanger the unity of minds, because unity of minds is the lifeline of our country, and makes our country truly unique. After all what is justice, what is democracy? Every citizen in the country has a right to live with dignity; every citizen has a right to aspire for distinction. To access the large number of opportunities, through just and fair means, in order to attain that dignity and distinction is what democracy is all about. That is what our Constitution is all about. And that is what makes life wholesome and worth living in a true and vibrant democracy, the essence of which is tolerance for people's belief systems and lifestyles.

I believe that it is necessary for all of us to work for unity of minds. The increasing intolerance for the views of others and increasing contempt for the way of life or religion of others, or the expression of these differences through lawless violence against people cannot be justified in any context. All of us have to work hard and do everything to protect the rights of every individual. That is the very foundation of the democratic values which I believe are our civilizational heritage and the very soul of our nation.

After I finished my two-day tour, the media wanted a message from me, for which a press meet was organized. I expressed my thoughts through a statement in which I urged the need for an intensified movement to completely eliminate communal and other forms of strife and bring about unity of minds.

Each individual has the fundamental right to practice his religious, cultural and language faith. We cannot do anything to disturb that.

10

AT HOME ABROAD

I am a world citizen,
Every citizen is my own kith and kin.

I have not been much of a foreign traveller as my hands were always full with time-bound national tasks throughout my professional career. As the first citizen of the country, however, receiving heads of state in India and honouring our own commitments by visiting foreign countries were official requirements. Whenever foreign delegations visited, the enthusiastic Rashtrapati Bhavan team worked hard to shower them with hospitality and present the accomplishments of our country. For me, the most important aspect of these visits was how to present the core competencies of our country and how to learn from the practices of other countries for our benefit. From this was born the concept of the World Knowledge Platform, which I developed in discussion with many specialists and dignitaries. We shared our concerns on environmental degradation and discussed the necessity of energy independence. We showed visitors Indian capabilities in IT, e-governance and pharmaceuticals. I was happy that every meeting or visit was geared towards implementing some mutually beneficial bilateral or multilateral programme.

Each of my visits abroad was important in its own way. In Sudan, discussions centred on building an oil pipeline from the southern part of the country to the capital Khartoum costing nearly a billion dollars in which India would cooperate. Today oil is flowing from Sudan to India. In Ukraine there was a very hectic programme. The visit resulted in advances in space cooperation. However, I give only a few highlights of those journeys. I went to South Africa in September 2004. President Thabo Mbeki requested that I address the Pan African Parliament, representing fifty-three African countries, in Johannesburg. I gladly accepted the request and as my team and I prepared for my speech, we pondered what we could offer to connect the African nations with India's core competencies. This led to the emergence of the concept of the Pan African e-Network, which would provide education, health care and e-governance services from twelve universities and seventeen specialty hospitals from India and Africa and also connect all the presidents of the Pan African nations to enable smooth exchange of ideas between them.

The initial budgetary estimates by experts indicated that it would cost $50 million to $100 million to establish the e-Network. Before presenting the proposal to the Pan African Parliament, I briefed the prime minister, Dr Manmohan Singh, who felt that the proposal was in tune with the Focus Africa theme of the Government of India and would be a useful tool for cooperation between the Pan African countries and India.

The Pan African e-Network Project, which has now achieved considerable momentum, was formally inaugurated by the Government of India on 26 February 2009. Today, the e-Network has become a good example of fulfilling international social responsibility.

I think it was in 2006 that the president of the European Parliament, Josep Borrell Fontelles, called on me at Rashtrapati Bhavan. During our discussions, he talked to me at length about a topic that is close to my heart, the Evolution of Enlightened Citizens, which he had read about on my website. He asked me numerous questions on the subject. The questions were thoughtful, deep and purposeful. After our discussion, he invited me to address the European Parliament, which had 785 members representing twenty-seven member states of the European Union. The parliament is the only directly elected body of the European Union. He also requested that I address the parliament before his term as president ended in December 2006. However, because of my various commitments during 2006, I was unable to give the address till 25 April 2007. By that time Hans-Gert Pöttering had taken over as president from Fontcllcs.

As the address was an important one, I started preparing well before the commencement of my tour. I had several brainstorming sessions with friends, intellectuals, political leaders, scientists and the youth. I also composed a poem, 'Message from Mother Earth', especially for the occasion. The poem is a reflection on how the European nations, which went through many brutal wars as they fought one another, successfully converged to form the European Union with a focus on the economic development, prosperity, peace and happiness of all the member nations. It is indeed a pioneering initiative in regional cooperation.

When I reached the European Parliament on the morning of 25 April, I was welcomed by the president and his colleagues. It made for an impressive sight to see the 785 representatives of the European Union, and the overflowing visitor's gallery.

My address on the occasion, titled 'Dynamics of Unity of Nations', emphasized the need for a confluence of civilizations, based on India's historical experience, instead of a conflict of civilizations. My speech highlighted the evolution of enlightened citizenship, which has three components: education with a value system; religion transforming into spirituality; and societal transformation through national development. I also spoke on the necessity of achieving energy independence in India and Europe and outlined a mechanism for its realization. My lecture was cheered periodically. At the end of my address, I recited the poem that I had composed specifically for the occasion, with the permission of all the members.

MESSAGE FROM MOTHER EARTH

Beautiful environment leads
To beautiful minds;
Beautiful minds generate,
Freshness and creativity.

Created explorers of land and sea,
Created minds that innovate,
Created great scientific minds,
Created everywhere, why?

Gave birth to many discoveries,
Discovered a continent and unknown lands,
Ventured into unexplored paths,
Created new highways.

In the minds of the best,
Worst was also born;
Generated seeds of battle and hatred,
Hundreds of years of wars and blood.

Millions of my wonderful children,
Lost in the land and sea;
Tears flooded many nations,
Many engulfed in ocean of sadness.
Then, then came, the vision of European Union,
Took the oath,
Never to turn human knowledge,
Against ourselves or others.

United in their thinking,
Actions emanated,

To make Europe prosperous and peaceful,
Born, the European Union.

Those glad tidings captivated
The people everywhere.
Oh! European Union, let your missions,
Spread everywhere, like the air we breathe.

As I completed reading my poem, I was touched by the moving and spontaneous response from every member of the parliament. The standing ovation I received was indeed a tribute to our nation. In response, I conveyed the greetings of the one billion people of India to the citizens of the European Union countries. During his concluding remarks after my address, President Pöttering said, I quote, 'Mr President Abdul Kalam, in the name of European Parliament, I want to thank you for this most important and inspiring speech. This was one of the extraordinary speeches we have ever heard from a statesman, scientist and a poet. This is unique. All the best to this great nation India, all the best to our cooperation between the great nation India and the European Union, all the best Mr President.'

After my address, many members wanted to discuss specific aspects of the speech with me. The general observation was that India is a great nation and is rich in human values.

I consider my address at the European Parliament as a very important one in the context of promoting unity of minds throughout the world. My address was quoted in many countries and reached a global audience through numerous websites, including YouTube.

After I returned to India, I addressed Parliament and expressed the European Union's willingness to work on a number of missions such as energy independence and building a World Knowledge Platform, so that India could take these initiatives forward.

∼

When I went to Greece, I made a special trip to Socrates' cave. People rarely go to this cave because it is in a hilly and difficult region. At my request, a visit was arranged. When I went there, I spent a few minutes in the cave with only a flickering light that I was given. I was alone for these five minutes. I was in a meditative mood. I wondered why Socrates, one of the greatest thinkers of the world, swallowed poison to take his own life. I remembered his words that the value of what he preached was more important than his life. Suddenly in that dark cave, one could see like a bright light the legacy of reason that he left to the world.

∼

I went to Switzerland in 2005. When I landed, a surprise was awaiting me. The vice president, after receiving me, said that his country had declared 26 May 2005 as Science Day to commemorate my visit. This was indeed an unexpected gesture on the part of the Swiss government. When I met the president, I thanked him for it. He told me that he had read two of my books, *Ignited Minds* and *India 2020*. Impressed, he had briefed his cabinet on my accomplishments in space and defence science and the cabinet decided to celebrate my visit to Switzerland by declaring a Science Day. I had the opportunity while there to visit scientific laboratories and meet with researchers, students and academics. I also went to the Swiss Federal Institute of Technology, Zurich, which was where Einstein first studied when he came from Germany. There I visited the Bose-Einstein laboratory where six scientists were working on Bose-Einstein condensate experiments. Here also I had the opportunity to address the faculty and students and talked on the topic 'Technology and National Development'. I concluded my talk with Sir C.V. Raman's exhortation to students, 'We need a spirit of victory, a spirit that will carry us to our rightful place under the sun, a spirit which will recognize that we, as inheritors of a proud civilization, are entitled to a rightful place on this planet. If that indomitable spirit were to arise, nothing can hold us from achieving our rightful destiny.'

∽

I cannot omit to mention Dr Nelson Mandela, whom I met in 2004. There are two big lessons one can learn from this great personality: The indomitability of the spirit and the virtue of forgiveness.

Cape Town is famous for its Table Mountain; it has got three peaks called Table Peak, Devil Peak, and Fake Peak. The peaks presented a beautiful sight throughout the day, as drifting clouds, sometimes dark and sometimes white, embraced their tops. We travelled to Robben Island from

Cape Town by helicopter. When we reached the island, we were received by Ahmed Kathrada, a South African who was a co-prisoner with Dr Mandela. It surprised me to see the tiny room where Dr Mandela, who is six feet tall, was imprisoned for twenty-six years for fighting against apartheid. A major part of his life was spent on this island. He used to be taken for quarrying in the nearby mountain for a few hours in bright sun. This is when his sight got damaged. In spite of the torture he underwent his spirit remained indomitable. In that small room, when the wardens went to sleep, he wrote what eventually became a famous book, *Long Walk to Freedom*.

It was a great event for me to meet him in his house in Johannesburg. When I shook his hand, I felt that I was touching the hand of a mighty soul. When he got up he discarded the walking stick; I became his support. There is a big lesson that we can learn from him. It is there in one of the Thirukkurals too. 'For those who do ill to you, the best punishment is to return good to them.'

My association with trains goes back to my childhood days, when I used to collect newspapers thrown from the train for distribution to Rameswaram town. Train journeys are a good way to see your land and smell its fragrance. Sometimes when the fog comes in there is a certain intimacy to the landscape as you see patches of fields and villages from up close. One can use the transit time to understand problems and find solutions to them. All in all, a train journey is quite pleasurable and I decided to activate the presidential train.

The Presidential Saloon consists of a pair of twin coaches that are reserved for exclusive use by the head of state. The coaches have a dining room that doubles as a visiting room, a lounge room or conference room and the president's bedroom. There is also a kitchen and chambers for the president's secretaries and staff as well as the railway staff who accompany him. The coaches are luxuriously appointed with teak furniture and silk drapes and cushion covers.

The coaches saw some use in the 1960s and early 1970s. There was even a tradition of having the president on the completion of his term use the coaches for his outbound journey from New Delhi to wherever he had decided to settle down. The last president to use the coaches in this way was Neelam Sanjiva Reddy, in 1977.

The coaches were not in use after that, an account of security concerns possibly, but maintenance was kept up. When I used the train on 30 May 2003 for a 60 km journey from Harnaut to Patna it was after twenty-six years that they were put to use. The coaches were renovated and provided with modern equipment such as satellite-based communication systems and I tried to make as much use of them as I could, thrice in all.

I made two other journeys. One was from Chandigarh to Delhi in 2004 and the third was from Delhi to Dehra Dun in 2006. These train journeys were necessitated due to uncertain weather and also because the travel time could be well used for meetings.

The journey from Harnaut to Patna became a multipurpose

journey. I laid the foundation stone for the new railway workshop at Harnaut. Nitish Kumar, who was railway minister, was very happy and all smiles at seeing a huge railway complex being launched in his home state. In my address, I told the audience at Harnaut that I was just arriving from an ancient site of learning, Nalanda. I hoped that Bihar would revive this great university with a new, contemporary curriculum that included subjects dealing with promoting peace in the world.

The train journey was immensely useful as I invited fifteen vice chancellors of Bihar to travel with me and discuss for an hour the problems pertaining to the universities in the state.

I could emphasize to them the necessity of the universities taking up courses which had direct relevance to the development programmes of the state. The governor of Bihar took a special interest in solving the problems which were affecting the performance of the universities and bringing them on a par with other universities in the country. After two years, I found that they had achieved the goal for conduct of calendar-based examinations.

There was a pleasant footnote to the journey. At the Patna railway station I saw Lalu Prasad Yadav, the leader of the Rashtriya Janata Dal, and the Janata Dal (United) leader Nitish Kumar, who had come to receive me, but both were looking in different directions. As soon as I got down from the train, I brought both the political rivals together and made them shake hands, much to the delight of the crowd assembled there.

On 5 January 2004, I went to Chandigarh for inaugurating

the Children's Science Congress and also to address the scientific community. I had to come back to Delhi for another important task scheduled on 6 January. To overcome the uncertainty arising from early morning fog, I used the train to reach Delhi in time. Particularly I enjoyed inaugurating the science congress where students from all parts of the country numbering more than a thousand had assembled with their projects.

The third time I travelled by train was in 2006. I went to Dehra Dun for taking the presidential salute at the passing out parade at the Indian Military Academy. It was winter and due to poor visibility in the mornings, reaching by air in time for the parade was uncertain. It was foggy at night too. The train went from the Safdarjung station to Dehra Dun non-stop, but the railways had arranged a number of checkpoints to ensure its safe movement.

It was pleasant to be among the cheerful graduating officers. Particularly, many graduating officers asked me questions on what type of India they were going to defend. To this group of officers, I related something that came up on a visit to some northern command units, very close to the border. The visit was being closely watched by the Pakistani army personnel across the border. There I addressed around two hundred young officers belonging to different units. After my address, before going for Bada Khana, I put a question to the young officers. Dear young officers, I said, since you have more than thirty years of service in front of you in the army, can you tell me what is the unique mission you would like to accomplish as an officer. The senior officers were silent but the younger ones lifted their hands. I chose one. After saluting me, the officer said, 'Sir, I have a dream. That dream is to get back all the land belonging to my nation which has been occupied by others.' The whole meeting was electrified and everyone cheered that young officer. When I narrated this answer to the graduating cadets, there was the same response: 'We will also do that, sir.' The train journeys linger in memory for these reasons.

One of the most beautiful sights I have seen was in Sudan, that of the Blue Nile and White Nile merging and being transformed into a different river, a different colour, much like it is at the Sangam here. In meeting people we are transformed too, though we stay the same.

11

REJUVENATING THE HEART OF INDIA

The village movement is an attempt to establish healthy contact with the villages by inducing those who are fired with the spirit of service to settle in them and find self-expression in the service of villagers . . .

—Mahatma Gandhi

India lives in its villages. It is from there that its culture, heritage, customs and philosophy of life emerge. I was born and brought up in a village; I can understand the rhythms of village life. In recent years the migration from villages to town has increased dramatically. All the migrants get is a tense, miserable life in slums as they try and earn enough to satisfy their hunger. Love and belonging is snatched from them. Developing the villages so that they can provide adequate opportunity for earning and improving amenities there can change the face of India, I believe. It will stop the migration to towns ending the misery of the migrant labour. From this thinking emerged the idea of PURA (Providing Urban Amenities to Rural Areas).

The development of any state requires the development of its villages. To gain first-hand experience, I decided to visit a rural area during my first trip to Bhopal in 2002. We went to Torni, which had neither a proper road nor electricity. As soon as I expressed my desire to visit this village, a number of actions were initiated by the state authorities. First and foremost, a several-kilometre-long all-weather road was constructed. Electricity also reached the village at jet speed.

During my visit, the villagers were very happy to demonstrate their achievements in watershed management and use of organic pesticides. I asked the district authorities to spread the achievements of Torni village to other villages in the region, so that they too could benefit from this experience. I also suggested to the state government that they create connectivity among a group of villages by forming clusters, which would not only facilitate the provision of physical connectivity in the form of roads and transportation systems, but would also enable the provision of common amenities like health care, educational institutions, storage facilities for perishable items like fruits and vegetables, and the creation of a food processing or other industry in the village cluster, which would create employment opportunities in the area. Nowadays the range of crop and wood-based industries alone has expanded to include a very wide array of products that are in great demand.

I also suggested to the chief minister and district authorities that they survey all water bodies in all the villages in Madhya Pradesh using satellite pictures, de-silt them and provide proper inlet and outlet connections.

The youth from the villages in the Torni area requested the upgradation of the middle school into a secondary school, which the state government agreed to do.

The visit to Torni village provided me with a field look at the various dimensions of development including the connectivity needed for bridging the rural-urban divide.

I was born and brought up in Rameswaram. Based on my experience there, I have often reflected how villages can be developed in such a way as to provide adequate earning capacities. My professional career has been in the larger cities but I have had several opportunities to visit villages in far-flung areas. When we were developing the India 2020 programme, one of its most important elements was that of developing the country's 600,000 villages. When my friend Prof. P.V. Indiresan came up with the idea of PURA, it struck a chord. I started detailed discussions with him and several other experts in the field who had a similar interest.

I was fortunate to come into contact with Nanaji Deshmukh of Chitrakoot PURA, Madhya Pradesh, Periyar PURA in Vallam, Tamil Nadu, and Loni PURA in Maharashtra promoted by a medical group. Above all, there was the Warana PURA in Maharashtra taking shape under the pioneering work of Tatya Saheb Kore. These experiences of rural development became the foundation for the evolution of the PURA system for the whole nation. As president, I have visited more villages than urban areas. The observations I made on these tours further helped in the establishment of PURA complexes.

When we engage in conversation with city folk, invariably many of them point out the present situation of increased pollution, fast pace of life, crowding and other disadvantages. Still they do not venture to go back to even their own villages. On the other hand, people of the villages even though they like their environment, leave their homes and venture into the cities in the hope of a better quality of life. Can we find a solution, so that village dwellers, particularly the youth, have opportunities to improve their earning capacity in the village environment itself? Simultaneously, can we make the villages attractive to the urban citizens, not only for holidaying and business, but also for potential migration. Such thinking formed the basis of PURA.

The government and the private and public sector in our country have been taking up rural development in parts. For example, starting an educational institution or a health care centre, laying roads and building houses, or providing a communication link in a particular rural area have been taken up in the past as individual activities. During the last few decades, it is our experience that these initiatives start well, just like heavy rain results in numerous streams of water for a while. As soon as the rain stops, all the streams get dried up because there are no ponds to collect the surplus water. For the first time, PURA envisages an integrated, sustained development plan with employment generation as the focus and taking into account provision of the habitat, health care, education, skill development, physical and electronic connectivity and marketing. The need of the hour is the evolution of sustainable systems which act as 'enablers' and bring about inclusive growth.

All of us realize that the development of villages is vital for a developed India. What is meant by development of villages? It means that:

1) The villages must be connected by good roads and wherever needed by railway. They must have other infrastructure like schools, colleges, hospitals and other amenities for the local population and the visitors. Let us call this *physical connectivity*.

2) In the emerging knowledge era, the native knowledge has to be preserved and enhanced with the latest tools of technology, training and research. The villages have to have access to good education from the best teachers wherever they are; they must have the benefit of good medical treatment and the latest information on their pursuits like agriculture, fishery, horticulture

and food processing. That means they have to have *electronic connectivity*.

3) Once the physical and electronic connectivity are enabled, the knowledge connectivity is enabled. That can facilitate the ability to increase productivity and find a market for the products, increase quality consciousness and interaction with work partners, help get the best equipment, improve transparency, and enhance lifestyle and use of spare time, and so we can call it *knowledge connectivity*.

4) Once the three connectivities are ensured, they increase earning capacity. By taking PURA as a mission, we can develop villages as prosperous knowledge centres and see villagers emerge as entrepreneurs.

The Periyar PURA complex has been pioneered by Periyar Maniammai College of Technology for Women, Vallam. I inaugurated this complex on 20 December 2003 and visited it again on 24 September 2006. This PURA consists of a cluster of sixty-five villages having a population of over 100,000 in 2003. It has all three connectivities, leading to economic connectivity. On each visit, I am amazed by the enthusiasm of the local population and the youth in making possible the integrated development of the cluster. The youth display their plans for development of this complex and their innovative skills. The initiatives have resulted in large-scale employment generation and creation of a number of entrepreneurs with the active support of 1,800 self-help groups. Two hundred acres of wasteland has been developed into cultivable land with innovative water management schemes. The Periyar Maniammai College, which has become part of the Periyar Maniammai University, has deployed its students and faculty members for the development of PURA by injecting technologies and improving the skill of the local citizens. They have also created a one-product, one-village scheme resulting in the selection of forty-five products from these villages which have met international demand. The close association of the education community at the grassroot level has enabled dynamic rural development in the sixty-five villages and also improved the lifestyle of their inhabitants.

Nanaji Deshmukh and his team members belonging to the Deendayal Research Institute (DRI) have created Chitrakoot PURA in Madhya Pradesh. The DRI is a unique institution developing and implementing a village development model that is most suited for India.

The institute understands that people power is more potent, stable and enduring than political power. By becoming one with the oppressed and depressed, one gains the acumen of administration and governance. Social advancement and prosperity are possible only by injecting the spirit of self-reliance and excellence in the younger generation. Using this principle, DRI has plans to develop one hundred clusters of villages having approximately five villages each around Chitrakoot. They have already developed 80 villages in 16 clusters consisting of about 50,000 people.

There is a village called Patni where the DRI has promoted

sustainable development based on indigenous and traditional technology, knowledge systems and local talents. The research work by the institute through field studies facilitates the development of a replicable and tangible model for achieving self-reliance in villages. The programme aims at income generation through value addition, innovative agricultural practices, inculcating scientific temper among the villagers, improvement of health and hygiene and striving towards 100 per cent literacy. Apart from development activities, the institute is facilitating a cohesive, conflict-free society. As a result of this, eighty villages around Chitrakoot are almost litigation-free. The villagers have unanimously decided that no dispute will find its way to court. The differences will be sorted out amicably in the village itself. The reason given by Nanaji Deshmukh is that if the people fight among each other they have no time for development. They can neither develop themselves nor the community. This message has been understood by people there.

I see that the Chitrakoot project is an integrated model for the development of rural India. It aims at creating a society based on family bonding, pride in Indian culture, modern education wedded to Indian wisdom, easing of social tensions, economic empowerment of all especially the womenfolk, health for all, cleanliness, concern for the environment, and equitable distribution of wealth among all the constituents of the society. This concept fully tallies with my view that developed India means not only economic development but also integrated development in art and literature, humanism and nobility in thinking and above all preservation of over five thousand years of our rich cultural heritage.

A welcome movement has commenced for understanding PURA and taking it up as a mission in different regions as a public-private partnership. I am sure the signal is very strong and India will have nearly 7,000 PURA complexes covering all its villages in the near future.

Gandhiji said, the real India lies in its villages. It is this vast mass of humanity that can help India make its full contribution to the world.

12

IN THE GARDEN

I build no walls to confine joy or sorrow;
To sacrifice or achieve, gain or lose,
I just grow flowers on all open spaces,
And float lillies on ponds and rivers.

When I was awarded the Bharat Ratna in 1997, Chitra Narayanan (the daughter of the president, K.R. Narayanan) took me, my brother and his grandchildren around the Mughal Garden. It was such an enjoyable experience that I expressed my desire to see the splendour of the garden during a full moon night. The president and his wife, Mrs Usha Narayanan, heard of it. From then on,

The president with jawans at an army post in
Arunachal Pradesh.

At a border post equipped with advanced surveillance equipment.

President Kalam
and Prime Minister
Manmohan Singh with
US President George W.
Bush and his wife, Laura
Bush, at the Rashtrapati
Bhavan banquet, in 2006.

Shaking hands with the president of the European Parliament, Hans-Gert Pöttering, after his landmark speech in 2007.

Kalam addressing students at University of KwaZulu-Natal on 'Evolution of Enriched Societies', in 2004.

Scenes from Africa: Meeting
students at a school.

Kalam's encounter with Nelson Mandela in 2004 left a deep impact on him.

Enjoying a fusion dance in Durban, in 2004.

Greece: Kalam with his team admiring the Acropolis, in 2007.

Paying homage to Mahatma Gandhi at Phoenix in South Africa, in 2004.

In Socrates' cave visualizing the great philosopher, in 2007.

Kalam addressing a religious gathering in his characteristic way.

whenever I attended an official banquet, the president and the First Lady invited me to stay in Rashtrapati Bhavan. At that time I did not realize that I was going to see more than sixty full-moon nights in Rashtrapati Bhavan.

In the time I was there, the Mughal Garden became a great experimental platform for me. It was a great communication medium between me, nature, and the citizens of the country; a place where I met people from diverse walks of life, including specialists in herbal plants, for which there was a section in the estate; the birds and animals that frequented the gardens became my great companions; and the serene and orderly environment of the garden and its magnificent trees gave me a sense of peace.

On several occasions I walked with a visiting head of state or government in the garden. A particularly memorable experience was walking with the heads of state of SAARC countries in 2007. I remember the prime minister of Pakistan, Shaukat Aziz, remarking that if we were to hold bilateral meetings in the Mughal Garden, differences between our countries would melt away. The prime minister of Sri Lanka said that instead of hosting a tea meet for an hour, I should arrange a discussion on the development of our regions in these beautiful lawns.

I installed two huts in the garden, both designed in keeping with the environment and using natural materials. One was built by craftsmen from Tripura and was called the Thinking Hut. I took many of my close friends to this hut for discussions during weekends and one of my books, *Indomitable Spirit*, was mostly written in this hut. The second hut, called the Immortal Hut, was surrounded by a grove of sixteen trees, a herbal garden with thirty-four varieties of herbs, a musical garden and a biodiversity park. *Guiding Soul*, one of my important books which explores the purpose of human life, emanated from the discussions I held with my friend Prof. Arun Tiwari in the Immortal Hut. Whenever a complex national decision was to be made, these two huts were where I sat and thought. Of course, the inspiration for many poems also came while I was there.

～

The Rashtrapati Bhavan estate is spread over 340 acres. The Mughal Garden is spread over fifteen acres. The garden is designed as three successive terraces, which are rectangular, long and circular in design. The rectangular terrace or main Mughal Garden has beautiful features like four canals, six fountains, a 70 sq metre central lawn (historically important national meetings were held on this lawn and the popular at-home functions on Republic Day and Independence Day are also organized here), 144 moulsari trees with umbrella canopies, beautiful roses and several lawns of different sizes. This garden is linked to the long garden, which forms the second terrace. The Long Garden has a 50-metre-long central path and a pergola in the middle covered with flowering creepers. On both sides of the path, there are rosebeds and a row of Chinese orange trees. The Long Garden joins the third portion of the garden in the west, which has terraced flowerbeds and a fountain in the centre. Because of the circular terraces, it is called the Circular

Garden. It looks majestic when the flowers are in full bloom. This famous lawn was the venue for the banquet for the American president, George W. Bush, and his wife Laura, and the delegation accompanying them. The grand success of this banquet attended by famous artistes, intellectuals and distinguished personalities was a highlight of the events hosted at Rashtrapati Bhavan. It was deeply appreciated by the presidential couple.

All the three terraces of the Mughal Garden along with the other gardens in the estate are at the peak of their beauty from mid-February to mid-March. Together they provide a stunning display of winter-flowering annuals, roses, different creepers, bushes and flowering trees.

Dr Brahma Singh, who was officer on special duty, horticulture, delighted in listing the variety on display. There was acroclinium, antirrhinum, brachycome, begonia, calendula, campanula, candytuft, carnation, chrysanthemum, celosia, china aster, cineraria, calliopsis, cosmos, clarkia, cornflower, daisy, delphinium, dianthus, dahlia, and so on all down the alphabet.

The beauty of the garden draws people in the thousands. The garden is open to the public without any entry fee. Special days are organized exclusively for special people like farmers, defence personnel, senior citizens, physically handicapped and visually impaired.

Dr Brahma Singh also brought out a beautifully illustrated book on the trees of Rashtrapati Bhavan.

∼

During 2002, I had several thoughts on how to add value to the Rashtrapati Bhavan estate by developing its landscape and creating additional green space. My experience in the DRDO with high-altitude agriculture and the development of vegetable and flower gardens in terrains full of rocks and stones came in handy. I consulted agricultural scientists at DRDO and in other organizations like the Indian Council of Agricultural Research and the Council of Scientific and Industrial Research (CSIR). Dr Brahma Singh assisted me and twelve gardens emerged thanks to our efforts.

There are very few tactile gardens in India and abroad. The National Botanical Research Institute (NBRI) of the CSIR in Lucknow has a tactile garden and its expertise was utilized for establishing the tactile garden in Rashtrapati Bhavan in 2004. It is also an elliptical garden and has a fountain and a stone-guided path, and houses thirty-four beds of aromatic plants, herbs, spices, fruits, and ornamental flowers. Each bed has a signboard describing the plants it contains in Braille in both Hindi and English.

The visually challenged were thrilled when they visited this garden; their pleasure was discernible on their faces. Every year when the tactile garden opened for the visually challenged, I would always be there with them.

The idea of a musical garden came up on a Sunday when I was in discussion with Dr Brahma Singh and my friend Dr Y.S. Rajan in the Immortal Hut. We felt the necessity for a musical garden against the backdrop of the banyan grove, the biodiversity park and the herbal garden. A musical fountain arrangement was commissioned in 2006. This project involved an exciting integration of multiple technologies such as digital electronics, electromagnetism, hydrodynamics, hydrostatics and human creativity. The fountains offer a spectacular show in which scintillating lights illuminate cascading jets of water in perfect synchronization with classical tunes, which can be either pre-recorded or live. On a full moon night, the twin fountains can be seen standing majestically in the garden radiating purity, perfection and glory, with the dome of the Rashtrapati Bhavan in the backdrop, the symbol of the pride and self-esteem of our country.

The musical garden had its finest moment one full moon night when Pandit Shiv Kumar Sharma played the santoor there to an audience of 500 people.

The biodiversity park was developed over the years by adding several avian and animal species, a waterfall, rockery, fish pond, rabbit house, duck house, a sick animal corner and habitats for birds. The park not only created a sense of caring and love towards nature, it became a source of attaining peace and calm. During my morning walk one day, I observed an abandoned fawn. My companion, Dr Sudhir, and I saw that she could not get up because two of her legs had been damaged during birth. Dr Sudhir treated her legs and we tried our best to reunite the mother and the fawn, but did not succeed. Every day, I fed the fawn with a milk bottle. In a week's time, she got up and started walking; as soon as she saw me, she would run to me for milk. After a few weeks, the deer herd accepted the fawn. I felt deeply touched.

I am full of nostalgia for my days in Rashtrapati Bhavan and the pleasure that the Mughal Garden and other gardens on the estate gave me. It was a pleasure that I tried to share with others – the musical performances which featured many notable artistes used to be held in the garden, for instance. I bow to the Almighty for his kindness at having given me this opportunity to enjoy nature.

13

CONTROVERSIAL
DECISIONS

Conscience is the light of the soul

It is hard to separate my thinking and actions done as president from those before the presidency or after. After all, the person is the same, and an individual's experiences form one continuum. There are three situations that deeply engaged my personal feelings, although the actions taken were based on logic and reason. The first one is to do with the dissolution of the Bihar assembly. I have discussed the issue many times but I will go over it once again.

A lot of advances in the IT sector took place during my tenure. Rashtrapati Bhavan became fully connected electronically. Wherever I was, in whichever part of the globe, I could access the database in real time from the files, and I could hold discussions. Emails allowed for instant communication. Thus when Prime Minister Manmohan Singh called me and said that the Cabinet had decided to recommend the dissolution of the Bihar assembly based on the governor's concern at the dynamics of the legislature what surprised me was that the assembly had been in suspended animation for over six months. Hence, I asked the prime minister, how come this sudden development had taken place. The PM said he would call back. The second call came at 1 a.m. Moscow time. I discussed the issues and raised the questions with the PM and I was convinced that even if I returned the Cabinet decision, it would not matter because the decision would be somehow taken. Hence, I decided to approve the dissolution.

As the court put it, in more technical parlance, 'the Governor of Bihar made two reports to the President of India, one dated 27 April 2005 and the other dated 21 May 2005. On consideration of these reports, Notification dated 23 May 2005 was issued in exercise of the powers conferred by sub-clause (b) of Clause (2) of Article 174 of the Constitution, read with clause (a) of the Notification G.S.R. 162(E) dated 7 March 2005 issued under Article 356 of the Constitution and the Legislative Assembly of the State of Bihar was dissolved with immediate effect . . .' Now the Supreme Court started debating the issue and many views emerged in the course of the discussion.

The Supreme Court in its judgement pointed out that the notification dated 23 May 2005 presented a unique case. 'Earlier cases that came up before this court were those where the dissolutions of Assemblies were ordered on the ground that the parties in power had lost the confidence of the House. The present case is of its own kind where before even the first meeting of the Legislative Assembly, its dissolution has been ordered on the ground that attempts are being made to cobble a majority by illegal means and lay claim to form the government in the state and if these attempts continue, it would amount to tampering with constitutional provisions.'

The Court put four questions:

1) Is it permissible to dissolve the Legislative Assembly under Article 174(2)(b) of the Constitution without its first meeting taking place?

2) Whether the proclamation dated 23 May 2005 dissolving the Assembly of Bihar is illegal and unconstitutional?

3) If the answer to the aforesaid question is in affirmative, is it necessary to direct status quo ante as on 7 March 2005 or 4 March 2005?

4) What is the scope of Article 361 granting immunity to the Governor?

When the Supreme Court started debating the issue many views emerged. I told the PM that the process by which I took the decision had not been presented properly in the court. I told him this once on the telephone and the second time personally. He mentioned that he would brief the lawyers to present the president's action supported by the facts and sequence of events in Moscow and the number of times we had discussions before I finally approved the dissolution. Ultimately I was convinced that the lawyers did not put forth my side of the actions as expected. The Supreme Court verdict was with dissension. Of course, the judges were supreme and they were placing the responsibility on the governor and to some extent on the government. After all the Cabinet is mine and I have to take the responsibility.

As soon as the verdict was known, I wrote a letter of resignation, signed it and kept it ready to be sent to the vice president, Bhairon Singh Shekhawat, who was a seasoned politician. I wanted to talk to the vice president and hand it over. The vice president was away. Meanwhile the PM wanted to see me for some other discussion. We met in my office in the afternoon. After finishing the discussion, I said that I have decided to resign from the post of president and showed him the letter. I am waiting for the vice president to come. The prime minister was startled.

The scene was touching and I do not want to describe it. The prime minister pleaded that I should not do it at this difficult time. He said that as a result of the furore that would be created, even the government might fall. I had only one person to consult, and that was none other than my conscience. Conscience is the light of the Soul that burns within the chambers of our heart. That night I did not sleep. I was asking myself whether my conscience is important or the nation is more important. The next day, I did my early morning namaz as usual. Then I took the decision to withdraw my decision to resign and not disturb the government. This action would have taken place irrespective of which party was in power.

Very few people in the country are using e-governance, which I consider a tool for a borderless world. It is a facility I use liberally in India and abroad. For those who move only physical files, it is very difficult to understand the power of e-governance. In dissolving the Bihar assembly (which was in suspended animation) I did what my conscience said was appropriate, regardless of where I was.

Manu warns every individual against accepting gifts. It places the acceptor under an obligation, he says, and leads a person into wrongdoing.

Broadly, the Parliament (Prevention of Disqualification) Act 1959, stipulates that certain offices of profit under the government shall not disqualify the holders thereof for being chosen as, or for being, members of Parliament.

During mid 2006, I received a number of complaints from MPs about certain fellow members holding office of profit. I had to deal with these complaints. I sent these to the chief election commissioner to study and conduct an inquiry wherever considered essential. When the complaints came in respect of two other members, namely Mrs Jaya Bachchan and Mrs Sonia Gandhi, a lot of members asked me why had the president initiated such an inquiry? Meanwhile I received the Office of Profit Bill from the Parliament for approval.

I studied the Bill and found that it had many anomalies. In the proposed Office of Profit Bill, I did not find a systematic approach towards deciding the question of what constituted an office of profit. Instead exemption was given to only the existing offices which were occupied by MPs. I also discussed the anomalies and my concerns with three former chief justices of the Supreme Court. I prepared a letter in consultation with my team and the three CJIs. I suggested that the Bill should clearly mention the criteria for exempting a particular office from the provisions of the Office of Profit Bill which should be 'fair and reasonable' and applicable in 'clear and transparent' manner across the states and union territories. Another point which I raised was in relation to the posts sought to be exempted by the new law. They said my concern was genuine and proper guidelines were required for determining whether a particular office comes within the purview of the Office of Profit Bill or not.

Then the question came up whether my letter pertaining to the Office of Profit Bill should go to the Cabinet or to Parliament. After going through the Constitution, I found that vide Article 111 it had to be referred back to Parliament for reconsideration. The Office of Profit Bill was not sent by the Cabinet for my approval but by Parliament. Hence, I returned the Bill to the secretary-general of the Lok Sabha and Rajya Sabha for reconsideration by both the Houses of Parliament. This was the first time in the history of Parliament or Rashtrapati Bhavan that a president returned a Bill for reconsideration. Of course the next day, my letter returning the Bill to Parliament became a lead story in the electronic and print media. It became a subject of very intensive discussion. There was tremendous pressure on me irrespective of party lines to simply sign the Bill.

I only understood the meaning of profit or gift as stated in *Manu Smriti*: 'By accepting gifts, the divine light in the person gets extinguished.' A Hadith says, 'When the Almighty appoints a person to a position, He takes care of his provision. If a person takes anything beyond that, it is an illegal gain.'

That was my concern and reason for returning the Office of Profit Bill. The Bill was reconsidered and sent back for my approval. The prime minister met me and he was surprised, as I normally send the approved Bill the next day. Why were weeks rolling by with no action taken? he wondered. I said some action is needed from Parliament and I have not heard anything about it. The prime minister said the Parliament has already decided on the constitution of a Joint Parliamentary Committee (JPC) for going into all aspects of the Office of Profit Bill as per my suggestions. Meanwhile, criticism mounted for the delay. Of course I was clear that the minimum requirement must be met before I approved the Bill.

Many delegations from many parties came to see me on this issue. I was on tour to the North-East and I was flying from Kohima to Guwahati on my way to Delhi. During my journey, I received a message that the formation of a JPC on the Office of Profit Bill had been approved by Parliament. Once I got the confirmation about the action by Parliament, I immediately signed the Office of Profit Bill.

After a few months, Parliament approved the JPC report

which was not complete and did not address the problem which I had suggested. Parliament has to deal with such issues with care, otherwise it would be construed that the highest body of the nation is promoting wrong practices which may set a national trend in different echelons of the government.

The return of the Office of Profit Bill clearly establishes how at the Parliament level, practices that cannot meet the standards of public probity are not debated and reviewed with the seriousness they deserve. This can be considered as a starting point for accepting wrong practices that will lead to compromises in formulating and practising a national standard.

Recently, we saw two fasting movements against corruption and many more may get inspired. I was asking myself, why are such movements taking place in our democratic country. This is basically due to the dilution of standards by Parliament itself. Hence, I would suggest that Parliament has to discuss for a minimum of two weeks the issue of corruption without walk-outs, and evolve a time-bound agenda for eradicating this evil in public life. As part of this, it would need to evolve a code of conduct for parliamentarians. If people's representatives fail in their mission, then the people who elected them may express their frustration and dissent in many forms. Each political party has to take stock of what they have done in their own way to prevent or eradicate corruption through Parliament. The time has come for both Houses of Parliament to deliberate on this issue of corruption and find a time-bound constitutional solution to eliminate this menace, which includes the recovery of money parked in accounts abroad. Such actions by Parliament in time will bring confidence among the citizens and promote peace and harmony in society which is vital for the accelerated development of the nation.

~

One of the more difficult tasks for me as president was to decide on the issue of confirming capital punishment awarded by the courts after exhausting all processes of appeals. As a substantial number of cases have been pending in Rashtrapati Bhavan for many years, it is one inherited task that no president would feel happy about. I thought I should get all these cases examined from a normal citizen's point of view in terms of the crime, intensity of the crime and the social and financial status of the individuals who were convicted and awarded capital punishment. This study revealed to my surprise that almost all the cases which were pending had a social and economic bias. This gave me an impression that we were punishing the person who was least involved in the enmity and who did not have a direct motive for committing the crime. Of course there was one case where I found that the lift operator had in fact committed the crime of raping and killing the girl without doubt. In that case I affirmed the sentence.

In my view while courts are hearing the capital punishment cases they should alert the law-enforcing authorities to intelligently find out the source of sustenance of the individual who is being punished and that of his family.

This kind of analysis may lead to the real person and the motive which has led to the crime.

We are all the creations of God. I am not sure a human system or a human being is competent to take away a life based on artificial and created evidence.

~

One of the responsibilities of the president is to appoint the prime minister of the country after every general election or whenever an occasion arises for change of the incumbent. On these occasions the president has to satisfy himself there is a party or a coalition which has the required number of members to form a stable government. The process of selection becomes more complex when there is more than one contender laying claim to government in view of none of the parties having a clear majority in the House. In this context, the 2004 election was an interesting event. The elections were over, the results had been announced and none of the parties had the strength to form the government on their own.

The Congress party had the largest number of members elected. In spite of that three days had passed and no party or coalition came forward to form the government. It was a cause of concern for me and I asked my secretaries and rushed a letter to the leader of the largest party – in this case the Congress – to come forward and stake the claim for forming the government.

I was told that Sonia Gandhi was meeting me at 12.15 in the afternoon of 18 May. She came in time but instead of coming alone she came with Dr Manmohan Singh and had a discussion with me. She said that she had the requisite numbers but she did not bring the letter of support signed by party functionaries. She would come with the letters of support on the 19th, she said. I asked her why do you postpone. We can even finish it this afternoon. She went away. Later I received a message that she would meet me in the evening, at 8.15 p.m.

While this communication was in progress, I had a number of emails and letters coming from individuals, organizations and parties that I should not allow Mrs Sonia Gandhi to become the prime minister of our country. I had passed on these mails and letters to various agencies in the government for their information without making any remarks. During this time there were many political leaders who came to meet me to request me not to succumb to any pressure and appoint Mrs Gandhi as the prime minister, a request that would not have been constitutionally tenable. If she had made any claim for herself I would have had no option but to appoint her.

At the allotted time, 8.15 p.m., Mrs Gandhi came to Rashtrapati Bhavan along with Dr Manmohan Singh. In this meeting after exchanging pleasantries, she showed me the letters of support from various parties. Thereupon, I said that is welcome. The Rashtrapati Bhavan is ready for the swearing-in ceremony at the time of your choice. That is when she told me that she would like to nominate Dr Manmohan Singh, who was the architect of economic reforms in 1991 and a trusted lieutenant of the Congress party with an impeccable image, as the prime minister. This was definitely a surprise to me and the Rashtrapati Bhavan Secretariat had to rework the letter appointing Dr Manmohan Singh as the Prime Minister and inviting him to form the government at the earliest.

Finally, the swearing-in took place on 22 May with Dr Manmohan Singh and sixty-seven ministers in the splendid Ashoka Hall.

I breathed a sigh of relief that this important task had finally been done. However, I did puzzle over why no party had staked a claim for three days.

During my tenure I had to take many tough decisions. I had applied my mind totally in an unbiased manner after eliciting opinions from legal and constitutional experts. The primary aim of all the decisions was to protect and nurture the sanctity and robustness of our Constitution.

14

AFTER THE
PRESIDENCY

See the flower, how freely it gives of its perfume and honey.
But when its work is done, it falls away quietly.

—Bhagavad Gita

I had a busy tenure as president. In the first year itself one of my goals was to travel around this beautiful land of ours and to go to all the states and see first-hand how people lived there, their environment and their problems, and get a sense of how happy they were. Lakshadweep, the small group of islands off the Kerala coast, is the only

territory I could not visit, to my regret. All the others, I
visited, once or more than once. Each region had its own
fascination. Underlying it all was a simplicity and warmth
that is typically Indian.

It is interesting to see how this travel was seen by others. I
quote from a report that appeared in *Outlook* magazine.
'Kalam is a peripatetic president who has already visited 21
states in the 10 months he has been in office. This is
possibly more than what most presidents manage to do in
five years. He packs in as many as 15 programmes into
these whirlwind tours, arriving the night before to fit in as
much as possible into his tight schedule . . .'

At the end of the presidency, I felt satisfied on two
counts. When I look charge there was a feeling of gloom
and despondency among students. I used to go and tell
them to be confident and try and enthuse them. No youth
need be afraid of the future, I would say, since India is
progressing well. India will grow and you will too, I told
them. Indeed, the growth rate has stepped up in recent
years. As the end of my tenure, the mood of the youth was
different. They wanted to live in a developed India, and
were willing to work for it.

People wondered how I would adjust to life away from a
busy schedule as president. However, before I became
president, I was deeply engaged in my writing, teaching and
inspiring the youth in national and international schools
and universities and participating in seminars and
conferences. I intended to go back to this routine. I had
offers for teaching assignments from Anna University,
Chennai; Indian Institute of Information Technology (IIIT),

Hyderabad; G.B. Pant University of Agriculture and Technology, Pantnagar; Delhi University; IIM Ahmedabad; IIM Indore; IIT Kharagpur; Banaras Hindu University (BHU) and others.

As I visualize it, from 26 July 2007 till now, my mission in life has been further enhanced. My teaching and research has now been well defined at Pant University. My focus there is on how the students can be a nodal point for India's second green revolution. Pant University is the first agriculture university in the country. It has a very large campus with a huge area available for experimental farming. At Kharagpur, India's first IIT, I have taught Leadership and Societal Transformation as a Distinguished Professor. At the IIIT in Hyderabad, I started teaching information technology and knowledge products, which are highly relevant for the India 2020 vision. At the BHU and at Anna University, I have been teaching technology and its non-linear dimension to transform rural economy. At IIM Ahmedabad and at the Gatton College of Business and Economics in Lexington, United States an interactive course was designed to introduce management graduates to the challenges of national and international economic development. The students offered a number of out-of-the-box ideas for development and the strategies needed to realize the ten pillars of a competitive profile for India before 2020. For example, a group of students is working to establish PURA as a public-private partnership venture.

I receive a number of invitations from abroad. Till now, after demitting office, I have visited, on special invitation from the academic, political and industrial communities, the United States, the United Kingdom, Indonesia, the Netherlands, Republic of Korea, Israel, Canada, Finland, Nepal, Ireland, the United Arab Emirates, Taiwan, Russia and Australia. During these tours, I visited universities and research institutions, attended industry and world youth conferences, and shared the mission of a developed India and conveyed the importance of partnerships with other nations for economic development and value-based education. So far, I have attended more than 1,200 programmes, meeting more than fifteen million people, particularly the youth. I have shared the dreams of the youth, how they would like to be unique, and their spirit and their enthusiasm for the great mission of development, combating all challenges. This venture has now been developed into World Vision 2030.

Each of these events has given a new direction to my life. When I look back, I introspect on what I have learnt from the change of course created by these events. Decision making in each case was complex and the events were chronologically very much apart. Still, I find aspiring for new challenges was the foundation for all the decisions. That's how life is enriched.

It can be difficult to find time for all the things one wants to do. In fact my schedule seems to have a life of its own. It is even more hectic than before, and I am thinking of giving myself a little more room. Just a day ago, I was good-naturedly ribbing R.K. Prasad, who manages my schedules and programmes, how come on return from Mysore on Friday I was fixed for Moradabad and Rampur on Monday, where I had four engagements before being driven back to

Delhi late at night, an address to the Pan African e-Network on Wednesday, and then Guwahati on Thursday, back to Delhi on Friday night and again flying out to Lucknow on Saturday morning for a conclave. A recent month's schedule, that for May, listing engagements, is as follows. The daily appointments, which can be quite a few, are omitted:

Schedule for May 2012

Tuesday, 1 May

- Visit Bokaro: Visit Bokaro Steel Plant and address the engineers and address the students of Chinmaya Vidyalaya
- Ranchi to participate in the launch of 'What can I give' programme

Saturday and Sunday, 5 & 6 May

- Visit Chennai and Trichi and Karaikudi

Monday, 7 May

- Meeting with 30 students and teachers from Govt Sr Secondary School, Chattisgarh

Wednesday, 9 May

- Visit Sanskriti Group of Institutions to launch the 'What can I give' programme at Mathura
- Visit Pagal Bawa Ashram – an ashram for widows at Vrindavan

Friday, 11 May

- Inauguration of the Technology Day Celebrations of the Department of Science and Technology

Saturday, 12 May

- Visit Azamgarh, U.P. to inaugurate the Vedanta Hospital and address the students of Azamgarh

Tuesday, 15 May

- Inauguration of the International Year of Cooperatives 2012 of the National Cooperative Development Corporation

Thursday and Friday, 17-18 May

- Chief Guest at the Graduation Day celebrations of the CMR Institute of Technology
- Golden jubilee oration at the Defence Food Research Lab, Mysore
- Visit to All India Institute of Speech and Hearing
- Visit JSS University and address the students

Monday, 21 May

- Chief Guest at the First Convocation of the Teerthankar Mahavir University, Moradabad
- Visit Rampur and address the school students of Rampur district
- Visit C.L. Gupta Eye Institute and address the doctors/ staff

- Visit the Moradabad Institute of Technology and address the students

Wednesday, 23 May

- Pan African e-Network address to the African Nations

Thursday, 24 May

- Visit Guwahati and address the Annual Convocation of the IIT Guwahati

Saturday, 26 May

- Address to Hindustan Times–Hindustan U.P. Development Conclave at Lucknow

As one can see from the diversity of the functions, each address has a different subject to tackle, and preparing the speeches is a task in itself.

~

The conclave at Lucknow on 26 May was held to generate ideas for the development of Uttar Pradesh. As usual I had spent some time preparing my presentation. I was happy to see that the points I made went down well with the experts gathered there and with the new chief minister, Akhilesh Yadav. At thirty-eight, he is the youngest chief minister in the country.

U.P. has the second largest economy in the nation and is

richly endowed in natural and human resources. With its 100 million youth, it is home to every fifth youth in the nation. My expert friends tell me that by 2016, out of every 100 skilled jobs being generated worldwide, about eight could come directly from this state alone.

My study of the economic profile of U.P. indicated that 73 per cent of the population is engaged in agriculture and allied activities, and 46 per cent of the state income is generated from agriculture. During the 11th Plan period, the state has recorded 7.3 per cent GSDP (Gross State Domestic Product), exceeding the 6.1 per cent target. The state has over 2.3 million small-scale industrial units. Presently, there are over 2.5 million unemployed youth, of whom 0.9 million are over thirty-five years old.

Keeping these aspects in mind, my presentation considered ways to raise the per capita income from the current Rs 26,051 to more than Rs 100,000 through value-added employment generation, promote a literacy rate of 100 per cent, reduce the IMR (infant mortality rate) to less than ten and remove diseases like leprosy, kala azar, malaria, chikungunya, dengue and TB from the state.

I went on to illustrate how these goals could be accomplished to empower its 200 million people.

One of the suggestions was to make a skill map of U.P. This would mean mapping all the districts in the state with their core competencies in terms of skills across the fields of art, music, handicrafts, agro products and cuisine, among others, and then developing their potential in a focused way.

There were many other specific measures in the presentation. My wish is that dynamic plans for faster development are implemented across the country to make the process interactive and result-oriented.

The 123 Agreement signed between the United States and India is known as the Indo-US nuclear deal. Under this agreement India agreed to separate its civil and military nuclear facilities and to place all its civil nuclear facilities under International Atomic Energy Agency (IAEA) safeguards. In exchange, the United States agreed to work towards *full* civil nuclear cooperation with India. After prolonged negotiations the UPA (United Progressive Alliance) government had to face a trust vote on 22 July 2008 before signing the safeguards agreement with the IAEA.

The crucial element in this trust vote was the Left parties who were supporting the UPA government from outside. They refused to be a party to the agreement. The president of the Samajwadi Party, Mulayam Singh Yadav, and his senior aide Amar Singh were in two minds about the nuclear deal and whether they should extend their support. They were not sure whether the deal would be favourable to India or was being done purely on business considerations by the West, particularly the United States. To clarify the position both Mulayam Singh and Amar Singh desired to meet me at my residence at 10 Rajaji Marg and discuss the merits and demerits of India signing the deal. I told them that in the long run, India has to become self-reliant in thorium-based nuclear reactors. That means, we will have clean and abundant energy for all our development tasks without any strings. The deal will help us to tide over the present shortages with respect to uranium.

One other important issue which came up is the agitation on continuing with nuclear power plants, especially the power plant under construction at Koodankulam in Tamil Nadu, after the tsunami devastation in Fukushima, Japan in March 2011. The agitators belonging to the local villages supported by national and international NGOs were demanding that the work in Koodankulam should immediately stop and they were preventing the engineers from proceeding with the work. Looking at the seriousness of the situation I carried out a detailed study of the safety systems of nuclear power plants in India and the desirability of going ahead with them and published an article in the English-language and regional newspapers explaining why this technology was so essential for the development needs of India.

Simultaneously, I visited Koodankulam with my team to review the 2,000 MW, third-generation-plus plant. I wanted to understand the plant's safety features and how it was addressing the concerns of the people which had been highlighted in the aftermath of the Fukushima event. I spent the whole day there meeting scientists and experts and the local people and also studying the various facilities of the plant first-hand. I was heartened to note that it is equipped with the latest technologies when it comes to safety. There are four important aspects of safety in nuclear power plants: Structural integrity safety, thermal hydraulic safety, radiation safety and neutronic safety, and it met the requirements of all four.

Later, I suggested that there should be a special PURA complex adjoining the villages around the plant which would help with education, training facilities and enabling value-added employment for the local population.

I am happy to see that these measures are being implemented and the government has announced that 2 per cent of the profit generated by the power plant is to be allocated for social welfare, rural uplift and enhanced empowerment of the citizens of the Koodankulam region. The functioning of the plant would be part of meeting the goals of energy independence.

The last five years have given me an opportunity to meet millions of children, pursue academics and research in multiple universities both in India and abroad, be a teacher in societal transformation to a large number of management students and contribute my views on pressing national issues. Above all, I was able to catalyse the introduction of life-saving systems in over eight states through the Emergency Trauma Management Programme.

EPILOGUE

Oh! Parliamentarians, the sculptors of Mother India,
Lead us to light, enrich our lives.
Your honest toil is our guiding light,
If you work hard, we all can prosper.

In 2007, as I demitted office, I gave a speech to parliamentarians that I feel has great relevance to all that I have said in the foregoing pages, and gives some points that need to be kept in mind. India's democratic experience as a free nation has been a phenomenal act of faith. When universal suffrage was adopted in 1951 there was no precedent anywhere in the world where millions of illiterate and property-less people were enfranchised overnight, with the hope that this would produce a quiet and steady social revolution, ensure to all its citizens the extensive list of rights promised to them under the Constitution; bring about a greater sense of national unity; and ensure national security , well-being, and prosperity more than at any time in its history of centuries of crushing alien rule.

As a nation, we have made significant gains in our economic performance, especially in recent years, compared to the historical past. Our successes however are mixed in nature, because our performance on a range of human development and governance indicators has still a long way to go. A new vision and visionary leaders are needed to restore a national sense of missionary zeal to fight for our people, for, by doing so, we are fighting for the world.

Parliament is undoubtedly India's premier institution, the very embodiment of representative democracy. Parliamentary democracy as a process of governance and a system of national politics has shown great purpose in loosening the historical power structures of Indian society, in sustaining free institutions, and in widening the scope of democratic participation. However, there is little doubt that, at the dawn of the twenty-first century, Parliament as an institution faces greater challenges than ever before since its creation in 1951, especially on matters related to human development and governance.

But what we have to see very clearly is that the effectiveness of Parliament as an institutional instrument of governance, and its capacity to deliberate, produce legislation and provide visionary leadership to the government and the nation, is increasingly dependent upon the functioning of a multiplicity of political parties, their capacities and calculations, *rather than Parliament itself as an institution.* That is the main reason why I consider it important to share with you the challenges facing the nation, including Parliament as an institution, and suggest ways forward to make India a developed nation by 2020.

There is a general feeling and appreciation that the environment internal and external to India's system of governance has gone through rapid and apparently irreversible change, especially over the last two decades. The challenges posed to national sovereignty, integrity and economic growth posed by these environmental changes need to be addressed coherently and rapidly. With the passage of time, along with increase in size and complexity, social organizations tend to deteriorate and become crisis prone. As a social entity, India's system of governance appears to have entered a stage of crisis, and this is a clarion call for self-renewal and change.

India is fortunate in having leaders of high ability, competence and vision in government and Parliament. It can also be rightly proud of its multifarious achievements in economic, social and political fields since Independence. Many predict that by 2050, India will become one of the dominant economies of the world. But neither democracy nor economic resurgence can be taken for granted. Constant vigilance is the price of liberty. It is important that democratic processes and functioning, however satisfactory they may appear to be on the surface, cannot be, and should not be, frozen in time. We cannot rest content with past achievements, and ignore recent developments that call for a change in the way we run our society and nation. Economic renewal and positive growth impulses after liberalization are occurring largely outside the governmental and public sectors, and the greatest challenge before us is to re-energize and give a new charter of life to our public institutions.

In the government and public sector, we need marked improvement at all levels not only in terms of output, profits and public savings, but also in provision of vital public services in the fields of education, health, water and transport. Many eminent scholars have also studied the functioning of Parliament, and identified the wide variety of institutional challenges facing the Indian Parliament. I have reviewed them carefully, and shall voice some of their important observations and concerns.

There is an all-pervading feeling in the nation that the time is ripe for improvement in the effectiveness of Parliament as an institution of accountability and oversight. Parliament can use many instruments for ensuring accountability of governmental performance, such as motions on the floor, oversight powers, and the committee system. But these instruments increasingly need rejuvenation. The fact that the Indian economy is globalizing has strengthened our economy. The nation is richer, but great vigilance is needed to enhance the power of Parliament in two respects. Much of economic decision making is now increasingly governed by international treaties, and the *Indian Parliament is one of the few parliaments in the world that does not have a system of effective treaty oversight in place.* These treaties are by and large a fait accompli by the time they come to Parliament. Hence the power to oversee and legislate on treaties and agreements with foreign nations is urgently required for Parliament.

The Indian state, like many other states, is restructuring

its regulatory framework with more powers being delegated to non-elected institutions. This process of delegation has been effectively carried out over the years, especially after liberalization, and this can, and has, increased transparency and accountability. Hence, to maintain dynamism along with parliamentary accountability there is need now more than ever to strengthen parliamentary oversight of these institutions; the executive is also to be strengthened by reducing their need to function by increasing the number of ordinances that are used as a substitute for legislation and weak financial oversight.

Day-to-day parliamentary scrutiny of the executive in financial matters is an area where greater emphasis and high degree of focus would greatly enhance the value of parliamentary functioning, and give much needed experience especially to the increasing numbers of the young and first-time members. The vitality of our parliamentary democracy has resulted in the proliferation of active participants, from five political parties in the first Lok Sabha to nearly fifty in the fourteenth Lok Sabha. The abundance of political parties in Parliament needs to be taken advantage of; and their functioning in Parliament has to be facilitated in a manner that strengthens both Parliament and the parties, thereby removing the barriers to collective action. These measures will soon narrow the growing gap between the complex demands that modern legislation places upon MPs on the one hand, and their capacity and inclination for attending to that legislation on the other.

Individual MPs doing good work in Parliament need to be consciously recognized and politically rewarded in their constituencies and within their political parties and coalitions. This will enhance the incentives for good parliamentary performance. As in the early days after freedom, Parliament has to once again become an effective voice on fiscal management, on the economy, on social policy and on the terms on which India is integrating into the global economy. There are no uncontrollable exogenous factors coming in the way of measures to strengthen the voice of Parliament, and encouraging positive, visionary leadership will surely encourage parliamentarians to shoulder new and challenging responsibilities for accountability and good governance.

Eminent personalities have made suggestions after several years of close observation of the functioning of Parliament. Some of them need to be considered seriously for implementation.

1. In the political plane

  a. Adopt measures to counter the threat of destabilization of a coalition government by a small party, in the same way as measures exist to prevent defection of one or more members from a particular party. A small party (with say less than 10 or 15 per cent of seats in Lok Sabha), which first opts to join a coalition and then defects, can be disqualified.

  b. All parties while in coalition should function under the banner of a single parliamentary party for purposes of parliamentary business.

  c. Ministries should set annual targets and ministers must be held individually responsible for the actual performance in relation to announced targets in Parliament.

d. Carry out constitutional amendment to enable a government with a majority in Parliament to appoint, if it so wishes, up to 25 per cent of members of the Cabinet from outside Parliament.

e. Public funding of elections should be introduced.

f. Legislation should be made that either House cannot be adjourned more than twice in a week unless the listed business has been completed.

g. 'Voice vote' should not be allowed procedurally to approve a Bill or legislative business. Counting of votes to be made compulsory.

h. The Speaker/Chairman is required by mandate to suspend or expel members who frequently disrupt the House.

2. In the administrative plane

a. *Centralization*: Transfer powers for internal security from states to Centre.

b. *Decentralization*: Transfer powers and responsibility for financing development programmes from Centre to states.

c. A Central Commission to be set up to decide on devolution of all forms of Central assistance related to approved anti-poverty programmes and relate such devolution to actual physical performance.

d. Specialized bodies need to be set up like UPSC for all appointments in autonomous institutions, regulatory bodies, and public enterprises, banks, financial, educational and cultural institutions in the public sector.

e. Reforms within government are made more urgently as the overall rate of growth has accelerated due to resurgence in the private sector.

f. New institutional initiatives urgently required for enforcing individual ministerial responsibility for efficient delivery of public services.

g. Planning Commission should be made responsible for placing before Parliament a report on actual achievements in relation to agreed annual physical targets.

h. A lid has to be placed on the tolerance levels of corruption at least at the ministerial levels.

i. Finally, in the judicial plane, reform of legal system can no longer be postponed.

As I have mentioned already, the emergence of multiparty coalitions as a regular form of government has significant implications for the working of India's democratic institutions. The role and effectiveness of parliamentary functioning has therefore proportionately diminished. Enhancing the majesty of the role of Parliament is essential, so that its functioning adds considerable value to the executive in the conduct of its business, through shouldering of greater responsibilities through parliamentary oversight. Hence, such reforms are necessary to make the Parliamentary system more viable and more stable to fulfil the high expectations of our Constitution. Above all, these concerns are overshadowing the urgent need to strengthen internal security to cope with global terrorism and domestic lawlessness.

Economic disparities during this period of high growth have widened. The role of ministers in governance has increased and hence it is imperative that their accountability has to be increased substantially. Care has to be taken that their wide discretion in exercise of commercial and other statutory powers does not lead to diversion and misuse of public funds. The system of governance has to be redesigned so that there is no mismatch between supply and demand for political offices at higher levels that could lead to increase of 'scarcity value' of such offices.

Encouraging parliamentarians to play a more active role in planning and implementation of socio-economic missions would result in the emergence of a wide base of parliamentary leaders and diminish the influence of those who enjoy a 'monopoly' in the use and benefits of power. This will also result in a situation of positive leadership that will deny opportunities of entry into politics of persons with a history of criminal offences and other legal violations. Engaging parliamentarians more effectively to coordinate between various institutions would ensure effective socio-economic growth and make certain that multiple agencies and government departments do not work at cross-purposes, that differences in views and policy approaches are settled at the right time and stage of project work, and decisions do not have to be taken at higher and higher levels for resolution. This would result in Cabinet committees and Groups of Ministers having to address really important matters where even empowered parliamentarians have been unable to resolve these. With frequent nation- and state- and institution-wide elections and short party tenures, the enhanced role of parliamentarians would ensure effective functioning of the administrative system as a whole and ensure that *the country need not repetitively face crises of governance.*

Parliament has now to emerge with a new vision and leadership to make our nation not only enlightened, united, harmonious, rich and prosperous, but above all, a safe nation, invulnerable forever to invasion and infiltration across its borders. I visualize the following distinctive profile for India by the year 2020, if the Parliament today resolves to implement the Mission India 2020 for a strong, prosperous and happy nation.

The challenges in realizing the developed India 2020 vision also provide opportunities for innovation in every aspect of governance and legislative actions. As we review the governance system and legislative processes for the twenty-first century, the full advantages and implications of technological revolutions, national and global connectivities, globalization and international cooperation and competition have to be taken into account.

The members of Parliament might like to debate these suggestions and evolve, with unified and harmonious leadership, a vision for the nation, in the same manner as when our Constitution was first drawn up. This twenty-first-century Parliamentary Vision for India needs to have a global and long-term perspective, and needs to be underpinned with implementation strategies, integrated structures and action plans for transforming India into a developed country by 2020 with National Prosperity Index as a measure and acquire energy independence before 2030.

It is this unique parliamentary vision and its effective implementation that would make our billion people smile. Working together in unity and harmony for a national vision is the greatest need of the hour for our parliamentarians. You will agree with me that this is one of the most important missions of our Parliament today.

The national awakening on issues relating to corruption, governance and others is emphasizing the need for Parliament to act with urgency and acumen.

AFTERWORD

There was always a feeling in my mind that what I have done in the area of nuclear weapons is against the ethos, philosophy and deeds of great human beings, till the day I met Acharya Mahapragya. Acharya Mahapragya was a fountainhead of knowledge who purified every soul that came into contact with him. It was around midnight, in October 1999, and Acharyaji had prayed three times with his monks for the welfare of the nation and the people. After the prayers, he turned to me and said words that still reverberate in my mind. He said, 'Kalam, God bless you for what you have done with your team. But the Almighty has a bigger mission for you and that is why you are here with me today. I know our country is a nuclear nation now. But your mission is greater than what you and your team have done; it is indeed greater than what any human being has ever done. Nuclear weapons are proliferating in tens and thousands in the world. I command you and you only with all the divine blessing at my disposal to evolve a system of peace wherein these very nuclear weapons will become ineffective, insignificant and politically inconsequential.'

When Acharyaji finished his message, a hush fell over the hall. It appeared to me as though all nature concurred with the saintly message. For the first time in my life, I felt shaken. Since then, Acharyaji's message has become my guiding light, and making it a reality a challenge that has given a new meaning to my life.

The action we took on the letter from a young girl that I quoted in Chapter 1 took a surprising, and pleasant, turn. The person we referred it to for help was a banker. He contacted the family. Together with them he worked out ways that helped them resolve all their financial issues. She got married and is happily settled. We were happy to know that our actions helped her achieve at least some of her dreams.

APPENDIX-I

Interview

I was interviewed by Manoranjana Singh of NeTV when I was in Mizoram after a visit to a number of states in 2006. I share this interview as it throws light on a number of issues, concerns and activities.

1. Do you also keep monitoring whether the state governments do act as per your detailed development missions of the states? Is there an effective monitoring mechanism?

I have given the road map using the experience I had through my visits to the states, inputs from the Planning Commission, inputs from the state government and the central ministries and independent evaluation. My team had spent sleepless nights preparing the presentations. I emphasized that the development of the state is more important and the state is bigger than the political parties. Also, I allowed discussions on the missions by the participating members. After my presentations, a number of state assemblies have conducted full-fledged sessions for discussing the implementation plan of the proposed missions. Also whenever I have visited the state later and addressed the universities, chambers of commerce and other business and service institutions, I have always referred to the missions and created linkages between the institutions and the missions of the state. For example, Karnataka, Madhya Pradesh, Bihar have taken follow-up action on all the missions and they are on the way to implementing them. In Kerala, the media also took the initiative and facilitated discussion with the government, intellectuals and other stakeholders. They have given an action plan for implementing the missions, thus, the media has become one of the partners of the state government. In the north-east, I gave the missions for Sikkim, Mizoram, Arunachal Pradesh and Meghalaya. These states specially have to give attention to harvesting hydro power and networking of water bodies and action to prevent damage to agriculture produce during bamboo flowering.

2. Is your road map an addition to the planned development as laid down in the annual and five-year plans? Is there any conflict between the two?

When we were preparing the road map, we asked for details from all the ministries, state governments and also the Planning Commission. We took the development radar prepared by the Planning Commission on an eight-point criteria. Our aim was to improve on all the parameters of the development radar and to integrate all the developmental activities leading to accelerated realization of goals. The missions that we proposed were based on the core competence of the state and were complementary to the state plan and the five-year Plans of the Planning Commission.

What we gave is a long-term perspective for making the state a developed one before 2015, since it is developed states that will make India developed before 2020.

3. Your intellectual breadth and vision and hands-on experience with science and technology applications have played a major role in framing these road maps. But does it not project a challenge to your successors in this august office that you have been holding with such distinction?

I personally believe any good system, irrespective of the incumbents, it will survive. What I have found in the past four years, there is a general awakening in the country about economic development. There are also some good successes. That is one reason, I think, a number of state assemblies have given me an opportunity to discuss the development missions. When I started with one or two assemblies, other state assemblies also wanted me to come and address them. I therefore see that the Indian people, Indian political system have started believing in the concept of mission-oriented development programmes for national growth. It requires a road map and an action-oriented plan, which may be fine-tuned based on mid-course performance review.

I personally believe, the President's Office has to have a professional team to generate the type of documents they prepared and presented to assemblies. Of course as you rightly pointed out it is a new initiative for the President's Office and is a very purposeful national mission. Also, this provides an opportunity to the president to be in constant touch with the needs of the citizens.

4. Though the Constitution sets down the presidential powers and the government's responsibilities, in the last four years have you found many areas of overlap, conflict

and grey areas in the relationship between the president and the prime minister?

The system is very good and resilient; it allows for plenty of opportunities to work together. When the tasks are executed keeping in mind the philosophy that the nation is bigger than any individual, there is no relationship problem. The two governors' conferences show the type of integrated working by the president and the prime minister.

5. One such area where the differences came up in the public was the Office of Profit legislation. How did you react when the Bill you objected to was returned to you, forcing you to sign it irrespective of your better judgement?

The issues connected with the Office of Profit Bill are quite clear. The decision we took was in strict conformity to the constitutional provisions both in letter and spirit. You will notice that the further actions by both the Houses of Parliament in terms of formation of the JPC and the general mood of the people and political parties vindicated our stand. I signed the Bill only after the formation of the JPC for evolving the guidelines for the members of Parliament on the definition of office of profit.

6. In your favourite area of science and technology and your remarkable campaign to wake up young minds to the opportunities in science, what new steps should the government take, according to you?

a. The entire primary and secondary education requires a revamping in terms of making children creative. Of course, the Right to Education Bill passed by Parliament was under discussion in the state legislature. Eventually the Right to Education Act will lead to the provision of compulsory and free education to all the children in the nation in the age group 6 to 14.

b. Major reform is needed in primary education. The expert team on primary education has to evolve a creative syllabus, creative classroom and above all deploy trained creative teachers.

c. Science and technology should be oriented towards realizing the India 2020 missions.

d. The university curriculum must create capacities such as research and inquiry, creativity and innovation, use of high technology, entrepreneurship and moral leadership among the youth so that they can contribute fully for India 2020.

e. Special avenues should be created for induction of about 1,000 young students every year to pursue pure scientific research as their career goal. Then it needs a science cadre employment opportunity.

7. For instance, while the medical and engineering and management training colleges are choked with applicants, many basic science courses go without students. Should there be some policy shifts to encourage people to take up basic sciences and research?

As you may be aware the government has started the Institute of Science, Research and Education in two states. We also need to work progressively to create a global human resource cadre which will provide the youth either with higher education in science, technology and research or with state-of-the-art employable skills which will make the country internationally competitive. By 2050, I visualize 30 per cent of the Indian youth will have higher education progressively compared to 10 per cent as of now and the remaining 70 per cent will have high quality skills in industry, service sector and agriculture.

8. The laudable decision of the government to invest Rs 100 crore in the IISc to create world-class R&D and teaching institutions is seen by many scientists themselves as very

meagre to achieve such a large aim. MIT and Stanford have many times larger resources at their command. IISc says enough doctoral students are not turning up in its research sections.

This is one of the initiatives of the government. There are other initiatives by the government with other universities and colleges; also the funding requirement for improving the infrastructure can come from multiple sources. With the suggestions I have made on science cadre, I am sure a number of youth would like to pursue pure research.

9. Despite recent claims in our science labs that India has done world-class research in several cutting-edge areas like nanotechnology, biotechnology, carbon composites, metallurgy, etc. but so far in the last sixty years we have not won a single Nobel for work done in the country. The question arises whether we are really doing world-class research or whether our work goes unrecognized for other reasons. What is your view?

Most of the Nobel prizes go to fundamental research. Presently, bulk of the money given for basic research is diffused in divergent areas. We need to unleash creativity among young students to venture into path-breaking areas of scientific research and concentrate on a few specific areas instead of diffusing the effort in multiple directions. I would suggest focused research in convergence of technologies using nanotechnology, biotechnology and information technology. India has a potential to make a large impact. Universities and higher technology institutions have to have core competence in specific research areas and funding. As more research professors and scientists are nurtured by the university environment, more research students will be attracted. It will lead to innovative research results and make an impact on indigenous technology. Some of the research may lead to award-winners. Here I would like to share an experience of how scientific magnanimity is a very important component in the research environment.

Scientific Magnanimity: Nobel Laureate Prof. Norman E. Borlaug, a well-known agricultural scientist and a partner in India's first Green Revolution, was receiving the M.S. Swaminathan Award at Vigyan Bhavan, New Delhi on 15 March 2005. Prof. Borlaug, at the age of 91, was having praise showered on him by everybody gathered there. When his turn came, he got up and highlighted India's advancement in agricultural science and production and said that the political visionary C. Subramaniam and Dr M.S. Swaminathan were the prime architects of the first Green Revolution in India. He also recalled with pride Dr Verghese Kurien who ushered in the White Revolution in India. Then the surprise came. He turned to scientists sitting in the third, fifth and eighth rows among the audience. He identified Dr Raja Ram, a wheat specialist, Dr S.K. Vasal, a maize specialist, Dr B.R. Barwale, a seed specialist. He said, all these scientists had contributed to India's and Asia's agricultural science. Dr Borlaug introduced them to the audience and ensured that they received a standing ovation. This scene I have not witnessed in our country before. This action of Dr Borlaug, I call it scientific magnanimity. Friends, if you aspire to achieve great things in life, you need scientific magnanimity. It is my experience that great minds and great hearts go together. This scientific magnanimity will motivate the scientific community and nurture team spirit and lead to newer discoveries and innovation in many research areas.

10. Do you think that presidential visits to various friendly countries serve any concrete purpose or they are just ceremonials of limited value?

Accomplishment in any of these visits is purely based on what India wants to achieve. I have visited fourteen countries and addressed their national assemblies and parliament. The visits have given a better understanding of each other and led to newer avenues of dialogue and cooperation. This will have long-term benefit for both the countries.

For example, I addressed the Pan African Parliament in South Africa. There I offered the setting up of Pan African e-Network at an initial cost of $50 million. You will be happy to know that the project is progressing well and has resulted in intensive technology cooperation between Indian teams and the African Union. This I consider as a major achievement.

When I visited Sudan, the ONGC pipeline project was in the offing; today the project has been completed by ONGC Videsh and it is benefiting both the countries.

The Philippines have decided to plant jatropha taking our example. They had invited Indian experts for working out their plans. Also an active cooperation has taken place between Indian and Philippine pharma industries resulting in people there getting medicine at affordable prices. NASSCOM has started working with the Philippines in the establishment of IT, ITES and BPO services.

As a goodwill measure, we agreed to treat a certain number of heart patients, particularly children from Tanzania. I am happy to say that all these children have been brought to India and they have been treated and sent back to their country. Simultaneously many Tanzanian doctors have also been trained in dealing with heart cases.

During my visit to Singapore and South Korea, I have proposed the creation of a World Knowledge Platform between the partnering nations. This programme envisages the design, development and production of state-of-the-art products using the core competence of partner nations in twelve different areas which can be marketed internationally. These countries are actively considering the implementation of a World Knowledge Platform.

11. Now that you have completed the major part of your term would you list some of the programmes which you have initiated and that have given you great satisfaction? Like the PURA for instance?

I would like to mention some of the programmes which give me satisfaction.

Rural Development: Ministry of Rural Development has planned to establish 33 PURA clusters across the nation. Several private educational and societal organizations are taking up PURA to develop rural village clusters.

Energy: Five states have gone in for jatropha plantations for bio-diesel generation. An energy policy has been announced.

Knowledge Grid: The National Knowledge Commission (NKC) is planning to establish the knowledge grid across the nation by networking at least 5,000 academic institutions, universities, colleges using 100 mbps network.

Virtual University: Three 150-year-old universities have started the Virtual University and I have inaugurated and addressed 20,000 students through virtual classrooms.

Village Knowledge Centre: A 100,000 Common Services Centres have been initiated by the Ministry of Communication and Information Technology (MCIT) to provide value-added services delivery to the village citizens.

E-governance: Establishing national ID and building e-governance grid for G2G and G2C services are gaining momentum. Government of India announced Rs 23,000 crore for the G2C e-governance services and setting up of SWAN (State Wide Area Network)

12. Do you propose to devote your enormous talent and energy and great dedication to some of your dear ideas after you demit office? Like guiding science research and teaching doctoral students? Would you resume your earlier work at the Anna University?

I will continue to work for realizing the Developed India vision before 2020. I will pursue teaching and research. My interaction with students and the youth will continue.

I also intend to devote substantial time every year in the north-east region. This is to focus on shaping developmental initiatives and enable implementation of projects which can make a good impact in a time-bound manner in improving the quality of life of people there and it will also offer a lot of opportunity for high-value employment to the youth of the region.

13. Would you also like to reveal what has been your greatest disappointment despite the great office you have held with such distinction?

I have great hope about the future of our country. I am only concerned about the pace of development. If all the stakeholders work in a coordinated fashion with a common goal by empowering the youth of the nation, we can realize the development goals of India 2020 much faster. Everyone of us should work with the spirit that the nation is bigger than us. I have the greatest confidence in the 540 million youth of the nation.

14. You have visited the north-eastern states and have advised them with road maps for their development. But

don't you consider such advice is not enough in a situation where there are many insurgent groups in almost all the states, the insurgency is preventing flow of investment and lack of investment breeds dissatisfied youth and that feeds the insurgent groups thereby creating a developmental logjam. Is there hope for the suffering people of the north-east in such a situation?

The north-eastern states provide us many opportunities and challenges. I also find that the people have started realizing that insurgency is working against the future of the youth. As aggressive development of the north-eastern states picks up, people will be ready to make sacrifices and meet any challenge coming in the way of development. Hence the message I would like to give both the state and central governments is to go for aggressive development programmes by empowering the youth of the state. We have to improve the employment opportunities through skill-enabling, knowledge-enabling and entrepreneurship development irrespective of the insurgencies and extremist violence.

15. What is your view on the opening up of trade, communication and road-rail routes to the east from the north-eastern states? Would that provide a stimulating influence on the economy and create more jobs and opportunities?

It is a must for development. The political system should facilitate such an opening up of trade, communication and road-rail routes to the east as quickly as possible. I have discussed with the state and central government authorities about the border trade development which can enhance the employment potential of the youth.

16. Will Rashtrapati Bhavan set an example in shifting our energy use from conventional to non-conventional sources as you are stated to be planning to do?

Presently, the experience in the country is only with the solar power systems of kilowatt capacity. What we are planning in Rashtrapati Bhavan is a 5 MW solar plant. The Ministry of Power and Ministry of Non-Conventional Energy Sources are actively working on this project for establishing the power plant at the earliest.

17. In view of the concerns over the energy situation would you be using your influence to promote such a shift across the country – solar energy, wind energy, tidal energy, etc?

As you have noticed in my speeches, I have been suggesting research in the areas of solar energy with CNT (carbon nanotube)-based solar photovoltaic cells for improving the efficiency of solar power plants. I am also suggesting nuclear power through the use of thorium. In the transportation area, I have suggested large-scale plantation of jatropha for bio-diesel generation. Our scientists are working on all these areas.

The visit to three NE states gave me the confidence about the potential of the states in biodiversity and specialized products in horticulture, food processing and garments. This visit also gave me lot of confidence about the inspiration of the youth of these states to succeed in life. They need to be provided with an overall vision of development. Simultaneously, there is a need to enhance the availability of communication and movement infrastructures which makes them remain connected with the external world that will make the states achieve accelerated growth.

APPENDIX-II

Mission Mode Implementation

In my speech before I laid down the office of president, I set out a detailed plan for strengthening Parliament. I suggested that each of the long-term objectives/goals, and other challenges that I had identified be implemented jointly by Parliament and the government, that is cutting across the boundaries of various ministries, departments and institutions, through public-private partnerships where required, in a time- and resource-bound manner characterized as 'mission-mode'. I hoped that the visionary leadership for each of these missions would emerge from the talented members of Parliament. In this way, all the members, cutting across party lines, would be enabled to take a real stake in effective governance. By taking ownership for specific missions, accountability would follow.

The Organizational Structure for Mission Management

Going by the typical model for mission management in advanced areas, I visualized that

- While selected parliamentarians would coordinate the missions, the Cabinet minister in charge of the concerned administrative department would provide directive leadership for the same mission to the required scope and extent within the boundaries of his/her ministry/department.
- The cabinet minister would delegate necessary ministry/departmental resources to the 'Mission Minister', who would then be made responsible to Parliament for the realization of annual physical and financial targets for his mission.

A conceptual sketch of a Matrix Structure of Multiple Missions to realize the India 2020 vision is shown below.

Mission-mode management would require about 15 to 25 per cent of a ministry or departmental budget to be decentralized and internally allocated mission-wise. Responsibility within each ministry for a particular mission would be assigned to a specific executive of joint secretary/director rank. The mission minister would thus have a team from several JS/directors from different ministries and focus them to accomplish the goals of the mission. Each member of the mission management team would be administratively accountable to the Cabinet minister, but functionally responsible to the mission manager.

It could be easily seen that comprehensive involvement of MPs in this way of 'matrix management' would require principles of organization and accountability as follows:

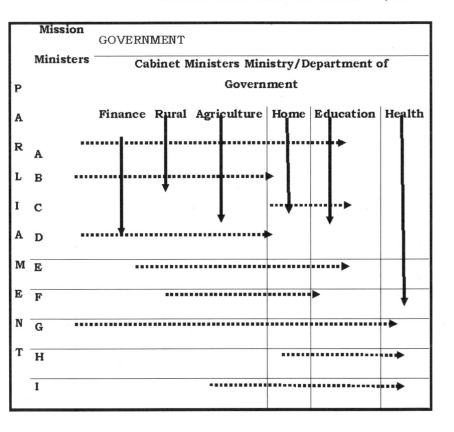

a. Mission ministers may be ministers of state or drawn from Parliament and even from parties not in the ruling configuration.

b. Vertical delegation of resources and powers by Cabinet ministers to mission ministers for specific missions, programmes and projects.

c. Horizontal integration of a specific mission by mission ministers across departmental boundaries through mission-management teams.

d. Planning Commission and each ministry/department would have to set up India 2020 vision planning teams for overall mission planning and resource allocation.

e. A comprehensive Vision 2020 plan would be carefully prepared by the Planning Commission with each ministry and mission-planning team.

f. Resources would be committed to missions from start-to-finish, and the life cycle of missions would extend beyond the life cycles of Parliament and government.

g. E-governance network would be used extensively.

h. Mission ministers would be directly accountable to Parliament.

i. Cabinet ministers would be accountable to the Cabinet which is accountable to Parliament

j. Large number of mission ministers would be involved in the India 2020 vision matrix, thus enhancing the role and accountability of Parliament; and increasing the number of high public offices for specific missions.

Democratic institutions are no doubt important in the functioning of a democracy. However, they should not be viewed as merely mechanical devices for development. Their successful use is dependent on societal values and on effective public participation in ensuring accountability of the governance structure. The time, then, has arrived for a national debate to serve as a catalyst for systemic change.

INDEX